काली पूजन
Kali Poojan

आचार्य विनय सिंघल
Acharya Vinaya Singhal

डायमंड बुक्स

ISBN : 81-288-1129-0

Published by : DIAMOND POCKET BOOKS (P) LTD.
X-30, Okhla Industrial Area, Phase-II
New Delhi - 110 020
: Phone : 011-51611861 - 865
: Fax : 011-51611866
E-mail : sales@diamondpublication.com
Website : www.diamondpublication.com

Edition : 2005

Price : Rs. 95/-

Laser Typesetting : R. S. Prints, Ph. 55136130

Printed by : Adarsh Printers,
Navin Shahdara, Delhi-110032

Kali Poojan
by : Acharya Vinaya Singhal Rs. 95/-

About the Author

Acharya Vinaya Singhal was born in a leading business family and was initiated into Spiritualism in 1980 by Swami Ishwar Das ji Maharaj, the ace disciple of Brahmaleena Swami Shree Satyananda Saraswati ji. Right since childhood Acharya Vinaya had special interest in Dhyan, Japa and Tapa etc.

By the time he entered adolescence his curiosity in Spiritualism, Vaastu-Shashtra, Astrology and Numerology became so intense that along with his university education he also studied deeply these occult subjects.

His abounding interests and talent made him display his knowledge through shows and other means which won him recognition in this field and he was awarded the honorific title of 'Acharya' by the 'Akhil Bharatiya Jyotish Sangha'.

Acharyaji's researches and investigations made him receive many honorific titles. He accorded due importance to the reality over the superstitious and collective conventional belief.

In this volume Acharya ji has vividly described one of the most important parts of Hindu culture, the origin of Goddess Shree Mahakaali, her many potent and success-ensuring mantras, Mangal strotra, her thousand names and her 'Kali Chaleesa' with a telling effect. We hope that this book would fill the (readers) life with peace, happiness and prosperity.

अनुक्रमणिका

Contents

प्रस्तावना

संपूर्ण विश्व को चलाने वाली कण-कण में व्याप्त महामाया की शक्ति अनादि व अनंत है। माँ जगदम्बा स्वयं ही संपूर्ण चराचर की अधिष्ठात्री भी हैं। महादेवी के समस्त अवतारों की पूजा, अर्चना व उपासना करने से उपासना का तेज बढ़ता है एवं दुष्टों को दंड मिलता है। नवदुर्गाओं का आवाहन अर्थात् नवरात्रि में माँ भगवती श्री जगदम्बा की आराधना अत्यधिक फलप्रदायिनी होती है। हठयोगानुसार मानव शरीर के नौ छिद्रों को महामाया की नौ शक्तियां माना जाता है।

महादेवी की अष्टभुजाएं क्रमशः पंचमहाभूत व तीन महागुण हैं। महादेवी की महाशक्ति का प्रत्येक अवतार तन्त्रशास्त्र से संबंधित है, यह भी अपने आप में देवी की एक अद्‌भुत महिमा है।

शिवपुराणानुसार महादेव के दशम अवतारों में महाशक्ति माँ जगदम्बा प्रत्येक अवतार में उनके साथ अवतरित थीं। उन समस्त अवतारों के नाम क्रमशः इस प्रकार हैं-

(1) महादेव के **महाकाल** अवतार में देवी **महाकाली** के रूप में उनके साथ थीं।

(2) महादेव के **तारकेश्वर** अवतार में भगवती **तारा** के रूप में उनके साथ थीं।

(3) महादेव के **भुवनेश** अवतार में माँ भगवती **भुवनेश्वरी** के रूप में उनके साथ थीं।

(4) महादेव के **षोडश** अवतार में देवी **षोडशी** के रूप में उनके साथ थीं।

(5) महादेव के **भैरव** अवतार में देवी जगदम्बा भैरवी के रूप में उनके साथ थीं।

(6) महादेव के **छिन्नमस्तक** अवतार के समय माँ भगवती **छिन्नमस्ता** रूप में उनके साथ थीं।

(7) महादेव के **धूम्रवान** अवतार के समय **धूमावती** के रूप में देवी उनके साथ थीं।

Preface

The great Goddess Mahamaya, instinct in every bit of the entire universe and its controller, has illimitable power and energy. The Mother Goddess of the world is also the presiding deity of the entire creation. The worship of her various incarnations enhances the worshippers' power and the wicked receive due punishment. The invocation of the Nava-Durgas (the nine forms of Mother Durga) bestows on the devotee great rewards and fulfils all his or her wishes. According to the Hatha-Yoga, the nine openings of the human body are believed to be the nine power centres of this Goddess.

The eight arms of the Mahadevi (Great Goddess) represent the five basic elements (Pancha Mahabhoota) and the three basic attributes (viz. the Sattvika, Rajasika and Taamasika) of nature. The Great Goddess's every incarnation is linked with the Tantra Shastra, which also reveals her supreme glory.

According to the Shiv Purana, the ten incarnations of Lord Shiv had these incarnations of the goddess. Their names along with Lord Shiv's names are listed below:

(1) In Lord Mahadeva's (Shiv's) **Mahakaal** incarnation she is associated as **Mahakali**.

(2) In Lord Mahadeva's **Taarkeshwara** incarnation she is associated as Bhagawati **Taara**.

(3) In Lord Mahadeva's **Bhuvanesh** incarnation she is associated as Bhagawati **Bhuvaneshwari**.

(4) In Lord Mahadeva's **Shodash** incarnation she is associated as **Shodashi**.

(5) In Mahadeva's **Bhairava** incarnation she is associated as **Bhairavi**.

(6) In Mahadeva's **Chhinnamastaka** incarnation she is associated as **Chhinnamasta**.

(7) In Mahadeva's **Dhoomravaan** incarnation she is associated as **Dhoomavati**.

(8) महादेव के **बगलामुखी** अवतार के समय देवी जगदम्बा **बगलामुखी** रूप में उनके साथ थीं।

(9) महादेव के **मातंग** अवतार के समय देवी **मातंगी** के रूप में साथ थीं।

(10) महादेव के **कमल** अवतार के समय **कमला** रूप में देवी उनके साथ थीं।

दस महाविद्या के नाम से प्रचलित महामाया माँ जगत् जननी जगदम्बा के ये दस रूप तांत्रिकों आदि उपासकों की आराधना का अभिन्न अंग हैं, इन महाविद्याओं द्वारा उपासक कई प्रकार की सिद्धियां व मनोवांछित फल की प्राप्ति करता है।

इस पुस्तक को आप तक इस रूप में पहुंचाने में कुमारी अंजली वत्स के सहयोग के लिए मैं उनका आभार व्यक्त करता हुआ धन्यवाद करता हूं।

— आचार्य विनय सिंघल

(8) In Mahadeva's **Baglamukha** incarnation she is associated as **Baglamukhi**.

(9) In Mahadeva's **Maatanga** incarnation she is associated as **Maatangi**.

(10) In Mahadeva's **Kamal** incarnation she is associated as **Kamala**.

The worship of these ten forms of the Great Goddess forms an inseparable part of the Taantrika and other worshippers'/aspirants' adoration of the Goddess and rewards them with secret powers and abilities as they desire.

I am deeply indebted to Ms Anjali Vatsha and acknowledge her contribution in helping me in this venture.

—Acharya Vinaya Singhal

श्रीमहाकाली की उत्पत्ति कथा

श्रीमार्कण्डेय पुराणानुसार एवं श्रीदुर्गा सप्तशती के आठवें अध्याय के अनुरूप काली माँ की उत्पत्ति जगत् जननी माँ अम्बा के ललाट से हुई थी एवं कथा, जो प्रचलित है, वह इस प्रकार से है—

शुम्भ-निशुम्भ दैत्यों के आतंक का प्रकोप इस कदर बढ़ चुका था कि उन्होंने अपने बल, छल एवं महाबली असुरों द्वारा देवराज इन्द्र सहित अन्य समस्त देवतागणों को निष्कासित कर स्वयं उनके स्थान पर आकर उन्हें प्राणरक्षा हेतु भटकने के लिए छोड़ दिया।

दैत्यों द्वारा आतंकित देवों को ध्यान आया कि महिषासुर के इन्द्रपुरी पर अधिकार कर लेने के समय दुर्गा माँ ने ही हमारी सहायता की थी एवं यह वरदान दिया था कि जब-जब देवता कष्ट में होंगे वे आवाहन करने पर तुरन्त प्रकट हो जाएंगी एवं उनके समस्त कष्टों को हर लेंगी।

यह सब याद करने के पश्चात् देवी-देवताओं ने मिलकर माँ दुर्गा का आवाहन किया, उनके इस प्रकार आह्वान से देवी प्रकट हुई एवं शुम्भ-निशुम्भ के अति शक्तिशाली असुर चंड तथा मुंड दोनों का एक घमासान युद्ध में नाश कर दिया। चंड-मुंड के इस प्रकार मारे जाने एवं अपनी बहुत सारी सेना के संहार हो जाने पर दैत्यराज शुम्भ ने अत्यधिक क्रोधित हो कर अपनी संपूर्ण सेना को युद्ध में जाने की आज्ञा दी तथा कहा कि आज छियासी उदायुद्ध नामक दैत्य सेनापति एवं कम्बु दैत्य के चौरासी सेनानायक अपनी वाहिनी से घिरे युद्ध के लिए प्रस्थान करें। कोटिवीर्य कुल के पचास, धौम्र कुल के सौ असुर सेनापति मेरे आदेश पर सेना एवं कालक, दौर्हृद, मौर्य व कालकेय असुरों सहित युद्ध के लिए कूच करें। अत्यंत क्रूर दुष्टाचारी असुर राज शुंभ अपने साथ सहस्र असुरों वाली महासेना लेकर चल पड़ा।

उसकी भयानक दानवसेना को युद्धस्थल में आता देखकर देवी ने अपने धनुष से ऐसी टंकार दी कि उसकी आवाज़ से आकाश व समस्त पृथ्वी गूंज उठी। तदनन्तर देवी के सिंह ने भी दहाड़ना प्रारम्भ किया, फिर जगदम्बिका ने घंटे के स्वर से उस आवाज़ को दुगुना बढ़ा दिया। धनुष, सिंह एवं घंटे की

Story of Goddess Kali's Origin

According to *Markendeya Puran* and the eighth canto of *Shree Durga Saptashati*, Mother Goddess Kali originated from Mother Goddess Amba's forehead. The story behind this origin is given below:

The demons Shumbha-Nishumbha's terror had enhanced so much that with their growing might they had ejected all the gods including Indra out of heaven and had captured it. The gods were running helter-skelter for saving their life.

During this distressing period the gods recollected that earlier also, when the demon, Mahishasura, had captured Indra's citadel, Indrapuri, it was Mother Goddess Durga who came to their rescue. She had also given a boon to them then that she would come to their help whenever they invoked her in their distress. She also promised that she would surely rid them of all troubles.

Recollecting this boon, they began to invoke Mother Goddess who duly appeared before them and slayed the powerful lieutenants of Shumbha-Nishumbha called Chanda and Munda in no time. Although a fierce battle was waged by the demons, eventually they were killed by the Goddess. Seeing his vast section of the army and the two prominent lieutenants killed, the demon lord Shumbha became very wroth and ordered his entire army to proceed to the battlefield. He particularly ordered the eighty-six demon warriors under Udayudha and eighty-four under Kambu Daitya to join the battle with their hosts. He also asked fifty warriors of Kotiveerya Kula (family), hundred warriors of Dhoomra's family, with the noted demons named Kalaka, Daurhada, Maurya and Kalakeya to go forth to the battle front. Shumbha himself left for the battle front with a thousand selected dreadful warriors. Shumbha, the cruel tyrant, also left for the front in a very ferocious mood.

Beholding the frightening demon army going to the battlefield, the Goddess twanged her bow so stentoriously that

ध्वनि से समस्त दिशाएं गूंज उठीं। भयंकर नाद को सुनकर असुर सेना ने देवी के सिंह को और माँ काली को चारों ओर से घेर लिया। तदनन्तर असुरों के संहार एवं देवगणों के कष्ट निवारण हेतु परमपिता ब्रह्मा जी, विष्णु, महेश, कार्तिकेय, इन्द्रादि देवों की शक्तियों ने रूप धारण कर लिए एवं समस्त देवों के शरीर से अनंत शक्तियां निकलकर अपने पराक्रम एवं बल के साथ मां दुर्गा के पास पहुंची। सर्वप्रथम परमब्रह्म की हंस पर आसन्न अक्षसूत्र व कमंडलु से सुशोभित शक्ति अवतरित हुई, इन्हें ब्रह्माणी के नाम से पुकारा जाता है। शिवजी की शक्ति वृषभ को वाहन बनाकर त्रिशूलधारी, मस्तक पर चन्द्ररेखा एवं महानाग रूपी कङ्कण धारण किए प्रकट हुई। इन्हें माहेश्वरी कहा जाता है। कार्तिकेय की शक्ति कौमारी मयूर पर आरूढ़, हाथों में शक्ति धारण किए दैत्यों के संहार हेतु आई। भगवान विष्णु की शक्ति वैष्णवी का वाहन गरुड़ एवं हाथों में शंख, चक्र, शारंग, धनुष, गदा एवं खड्ग लिए वहां आई। यज्ञ वाराह की शक्ति वाराही, वाराह कप धारण कर आई। नृसिंह भगवान की शक्ति नारसिंह उन्हीं के समान रूप धारण कर आई। उसकी मात्र गर्दन के बाल झटकने से आकाश के समस्त नक्षत्र, तारे बिखरने लगते थे। इन्द्र की शक्ति ऐन्द्री युद्ध हेतु ऐरावत को वाहन बनाकर हाथों में वज्र धारण किए सहस्त्र नेत्रों सहित पधारीं। जिसका जैसा रूप, वाहन, वेश वैसी ही स्वरूप धारण कर सबकी शक्तियां अवतरित हुई।

तद्पश्चात् समस्त शक्तियों से घिरे शिवजी ने देवी जगदम्बा से कहा-"मेरी प्रसन्नता हेतु तुम इस समस्त दानवदलों का सर्वनाश करो।" तब देवी जगदम्बा के शरीर से भयानक उग्र रूप धारण किए चंडिका देवी शक्ति रूप में प्रकट हुई। उनके स्वर में सैकड़ों गीदड़ियों की भांति आवाज़ आती थी। उस देवी ने महादेव जी से कहा-कि आप शुम्भ-निशुम्भ असुरों के पास मेरे दूत बन कर जाएं, इसी कारण इनका नाम शिवदूती भी विख्यात हुआ। तथा उनसे व उनकी दानव सेना से कहें कि 'यदि वह जीवनदान चाहते हैं, तथा अपने प्राणों की रक्षा करना चाहते हैं तो तुरंत पाताल-लोक की ओर लौट जाएं एवं जिस देवता इन्द्र से त्रिलोकी साम्राज्य छीना है, वह उन्हें वापस कर दिया जाए एवं देवगणों को यज्ञ उपभोग करने दिया जाए। तथा यदि बल के घमंड में चूर तुम युद्ध के इच्छुक हो, तो आओ! और मेरी शिवाओं एवं योगिनियों को अपने शरीर के रक्त पान से तृप्त करो।'

भगवान महादेव के मुख से समस्त शब्दों व वचनों को सुन कर असुरराज शुम्भ-निशुम्भ क्रोध से भर उठे व देवी कात्यायनी की ओर युद्ध हेतु बढ़े।

the entire sky and the earth resounded with its reverberations. These vibrations also charged the lion of the Goddess who started to roar loudly. Then Mother Jagdambika inflated the sound of her bell as much as to double the cacophony. The twang of the bow, the roar of the lion and the sound of the Goddess's bell grew much louder collectively to resound all the directions. That deafening sound pulverised the demon hosts a little but they surrounded Mother Goddess from all sides. Then with the intention of causing destruction of the demons and ensuring welfare of the gods the super gods Brahma, Vishnu, Mahesha, Kartikeya etc. adopted the form of the dreadful weapons called Shakti and reached near the Goddess. First to dawn was Brahma's seven-seated Shakti endowed with the Akshasootra and Kamandal. This Shakti of Brahma is called Brahmaani. Lord Shiv's Shakti appeared seated on the Lord's bull with the nascent moon on her head and decorated in the bangle on hand in the form of a ferocious serpent. This Shakti is called Maheshwari. The Shakti of Kartikeya appeared seated on a peahen for destroying the demons. The Shakti of Lord Vishnu called Vaishnavi appeared astride on Garuda and holding chakra (discus), the bow Sharang, a mace and a sword. The Shakti from Varaha, called Varahi, came in the form of a massive boar. She was so powerful that the mere twist of her neck caused the planets go helter-skelter. A similar shakti also emerged from Lord Nrisimha's man-lion form. Indra's shakti emerged astride the celestial mount Eiravat holding the Vajra with her thousand eyes. All the gods appeared in their shakti forms in accordance with their known image.

Then Lord Shiv accosted Goddess Jagdamba surrounded by all these divine powers (shakti). "For the sake of my happiness you should now destroy all these demon hosts." This request made a dreadful power emerge from the Goddess in a most ferocious form. Her voice echoed in such a way as if it gave the impression of bellowing of a thousand she-jackals. That dreadful power—the Goddess—asked Shiv to go to Shumbha and Nishumbha as her messenger. This duty also earned Lord Shiv an epithet 'Shiv doota'. She asked Mahadeva (Shiv) to tell the demons that should they want to live more, they should immediately return to their abode in Patal-Loka (nether world) after surrendering the rule of the three realms back to Indria so that the gods could continue to enjoy their

अत्यंत क्रोध में चूर उन्होंने देवी पर बाण, शक्ति, शूल, फरसा, ऋषि आदि अस्त्रों-शस्त्रों द्वारा प्रहार प्रारम्भ किया। देवी ने अपने धनुष से टंकार की एवं अपने बाणों द्वारा उनके समस्त अस्त्रों-शस्त्रों को काट डाला, जो उनकी ओर बढ़ रहे थे। माँ काली फिर उनके आगे-आगे शत्रुओं को अपने शूलादि के प्रहार द्वारा विदीर्ण करती हुई व खट्वाङ्ग से कुचलती हुई समस्त युद्धभूमि में विचरने लगी। ब्रह्माणी अपने कमंडलु के जल को छिड़कर जहां भी जाती वहीं असुरों के बल व पराक्रम को क्षीण कर उन्हें नष्ट कर देती। माहेश्वरी त्रिशूल लेकर, वैष्णवी चक्र द्वारा, कौमारी शक्ति द्वारा असुरों पर टूट पड़ीं एवं उनका संहार किया। ऐन्द्री के वज्रप्रहार से सहस्त्रों दानवदल रक्तधार बहाकर पृथ्वी की शैय्या पर सो गए। वाराही प्रहार करती अपनी थूथन से एवं दाड़ों से अनेक असुर की छाती फाड़ कर उन्हें नष्ट किया। और कितनों ने अपने प्राणों को उनके चक्र के द्वारा त्यागा। नारसिंह सिंहनाद करती हुई अपने विशाल नखों से अष्ट दिशाओं, आकाश, पाताल, शुजाती दैत्यों का संहार करने लगी। कितनों को शिवदूती के भीषण अट्टहास ने भयभीत कर पृथ्वी पर गिरा दिया एवं तब वह शिवदूती का ग्रास बनें।

क्रोध में भरी देवी द्वारा किए गए इस महाविनाश को देख भयभीत सेना भाग खड़ी हुई। तभी अपनी सैना का मातृगणों से भागते देख रणभूमि में आया दैत्यराज महाअसुर रक्तबीज। उसके शरीर से रक्त की बूंदें जहां-जहां गिरती थीं वहीं पर उसी के समान पराक्रमी शक्तिशाली रक्तबीज खड़ा हो जाता। हाथ में गदा लिए रक्तबीज ने ऐन्द्री पर प्रहार किया। ऐन्द्री के वज्र प्रहार से घायल रक्तबीज का रक्त बहते ही जहां भी गिरा उतने ही रक्तबीज वहां उत्पन्न हो उठे। सभी एक समान बलशाली व वीर्यवान थे। वे सभी मिलकर समस्त मातृगणों से युद्ध करने लगे। जब-जब उन पर प्रहार होता, उतने ही रक्तबीज और उठ खडे होते। देखते ही देखते पूरी पृथ्वी असंख्य रक्तबीजों से भर गई। क्रोध में आकर वैष्णवी ने चक्र द्वारा उन पर प्रहार किया व उस रक्त से और दानव उत्पन्न हो गए। इतने दानवों को देखकर कौमारी अपनी शक्ति से, वाराही ने खड्ग द्वारा, माहेश्वरी ने त्रिशूल द्वारा उनका संहार करना प्रारम्भ किया। क्रोध में उमड़ता रक्तबीज भी माताओं पर पृथक्-पृथक् प्रहार करने लगा। अनेक बार शक्ति आदि के प्रहार से घायल होने पर रक्तबीज के शरीर से रक्त की धारा बहने लगी। उस धारा से तो सहस्त्रों रक्तबीज निश्चित ही धरा पर उठ खड़े हुए। एक से दो, दो से चार, चार से आठ करते-करते सम्पूर्ण पृथ्वी पर रक्तबीज व्याप्त हो गए। देवताओं का भय इतने असुरों को देख और बढ़ गया। देवताओं

share from the Yagyas. However, "if they are drunk in the wine of their arrogance, willing to face me, they should face me and my 'Shivas' and the 'Yoginis' who are itching to drink their blood."

When the demon-lords Shumbha-Nishumbha heard these challenging words conveyed by Lord Shiv on the Goddess's behalf, they rushed towards Devi Kalyayani for ensuing the war. Maddened in rage they began to rain a variety of weapons—arrows, Shakti, Shoola, axes and pointed sticks called Rishtis—towards the Goddess. She took her bow in the hand and twanged it resoundingly and then used her arrows so precisely as to cut to pieces all those hurled weapons. Then Mother Kali merrily danced in the battlefield slaying the demons and trampling under her feet, their dead bodies. Meanwhile, Brahmaani would sprinkle water on the demons from her water pot to weaken their strength. Maheshwari came charging up on the demons with the frightening Trishool (trident) in her hand. Vaishnavi hacked off the demons' heads with her chakra and Kartikeya's Kaumari Shakti made a mincemeat of the demons. Eindree Shakti's thunderbolt (Vajra) blow made the demons' blood flow in streams. Varahi tore apart the demons with her physical might. The Shakti of Narasimha bellowed loudly to pulverise the demons to death. Some of the demons collapsed hearing the bellowing laughter of the Shiv dootis who swallowed them in no time.

This massive destruction of their forces by the Goddess and her assistants made the surviving demons flee in panic. Beholding this cowardly retreat of his 'Matruganas' there came forth the great demon called Raktabeeja. His quality was that wherever his drops of blood fell, there emerged more demons as powerful as Raktabeeja himself. Raktabeeja took a mace in his hand and attacked on Eindree (Indra's Shakti), Eindree also attacked with her vajra which wounded Raktabeeja. But as the blood fell from his wounds, there appeared as many Raktabeeja demons. In fact, in no time the entire earth teemed up with numerous Raktabeeja demons. All were as powerful and potent as the original Raktabeeja. In anger Vaishnavi attacked them with her chakra but more demons appeared again from the drops of the demoniac blood. There were innumerable demons all around. The gods got frightened seeing these emerging mil-

को इस प्रकार निराश देखकर देवी का क्रोध अपार हो गया। क्रोध के कारण उनका मुख काला एवं भौंहें टेढ़ी हो गईं। उनके इसी उग्र रूप को धारण किए चण्डिका के ललाट से 'काली देवी' की उत्पत्ति हुई। माँ चण्डिका ने काली देवी से कहा कि हे चामुंडे ! तुम अपने मुख को और व्यापक करो तथा मेरे प्रहार से रक्तबीज के शरीर से बहने वाले रक्त को और उससे उत्पन्न होने वाले तमाम महादैत्यों का सेवन करो। इस प्रकार दैत्यों का भक्षण करती तुम पूर्ण रणभूमि में विचरण करो। ऐसा करने पर रक्तबीज का समस्त रक्त क्षीण हो जाएगा तथा वह स्वयं ही समाप्त हो जाएगा। परंतु तुम रक्त को धरा पर गिरने मत देना। तब काली ने रौद्र रूप में प्रकट होकर रक्तबीज के समस्त रक्त को हाथ में लिए खप्पर में समेट कर पीती रही एवं जो भी दानव रक्त से उनकी जिह्वा पर उत्पन्न होते गए उनको खाती गई। जब चंडिका ने अनेक दानवों को एक साथ नष्ट करना प्रारंभ कर दिया तो काली ने क्रोध उन्मुक्त होकर अपनी जिह्वा समस्त रणभूमि पर फैला दी, जिससे सारा रक्त उनके मुख में गिरता रहा एवं उससे उत्पन्न होने वाले दानवों का वह सेवन करती रही। इस प्रकार रक्तबीज के शरीर से बहने वाले रक्त का पान काली करती रही। तभी रक्तबीज ने गदा से चण्डिका पर प्रहार किया परंतु इस प्रहार ने चण्डिका पर लेशमात्र भी वेदना नहीं पहुंचाई। तदनन्तर देवी ने काली द्वारा रक्त पी लेने के पश्चात् वज्र, बाण, खड्ग एवं मुष्टि आदि द्वारा रक्तबीज का वध कर डाला। इस प्रकार अस्त्रों-शस्त्रों के प्रहार से रक्तहीन होकर रक्तबीज भूमि पर गिर पड़ा। उसके गिरते ही देवी-देवता अत्यंत प्रसन्न हुए एवं मातृ-शक्तियां एवं योगिनियां व शिवाएं असुरों का रक्तपान कर मद में लीन हुई नृत्य करने लगीं।

❑❑❑

lions of demons like that of the Raktabeeja. The god's lapsing into despair made the Goddess further charged with anger. Owing to excessive anger, her face grew dark and the eyebrows a bit askew. This form of Devi 'Chandika' came to be known as Goddess 'Kali'. Then she told Kali Devi: "O Chamunde! Open your mouth as far and wide as possible and lick the blood drops that ooze from Raktabeeja's wounds before they fall on to the earth. Then you should consume all the demons by swallowing them up. This way licking their blood and swallowing the demons you move around merrily in this battlefield. If you do so, Raktabeeja's blood won't create fresh demons and then I shall end his life. But make sure his blood doesn't touch the ground." Goddess Kali then assumed a ferocious form and with a piece of the broken pitcher in her hand she continued to gather the falling blood drops and licking them in one swipe. Even the demons that were produced by the demon's blood on her tongue were immediately swallowed by her. Meanwhile, Chandika continued to slay the demons. Goddess Kali spread her tongue so wide that it covered the entire battlefield. Now the demons' blood drops kept on falling on it and she kept on licking them. Then seizing his opportunity, Raktabeeja hurled a mace blow on Chandika but she was not perturbed in the least. While Goddess Kali kept on licking Raktabeeja's blood, Chandika rained her many weapons on Raktabeeja to eventually kill him. As that demon Raktabeeja fell on to the ground dead, the gods and goddesses felt supremely delighted. The 'Matri-shakti' (female instructive powers) and the Shivas merrily danced all over the battlefield while drinking the blood of the demons in their sozzled state. This is how Goddess Kali had her origin.

❑❑❑

श्रीमहाकाली साधना के प्रयोग से लाभ

महाकाली साधना करने वाले जातक को निम्न लाभ स्वतः प्राप्त होते हैं—

(1) जिस प्रकार अग्नि के संपर्क में आने के पश्चात् पतंगा भस्म हो जाता है, उसी प्रकार काली देवी के संपर्क में आने के उपरांत साधक के समस्त राग, द्वेष, विघ्न आदि भस्म हो जाते हैं।

(2) श्री महाकाली स्तोत्र एवं मंत्र को धारण करने वाले धारक की वाणी में विशिष्ट ओजस्व व्याप्त हो जाने के कारणवश गद्य-पद्यादि पर उसका पूर्व आधिपत्य हो जाता है।

(3) महाकाली साधक के व्यक्तित्व में विशिष्ट तेजस्विता व्याप्त होने के कारण उसके प्रतिद्वंद्वी उसे देखते ही पराजित हो जाते हैं।

(4) काली साधना से सहज ही सभी सिद्धियां प्राप्त हो जाती हैं।

(5) काली का स्नेह अपने साधकों पर सदैव ही अपार रहता है। तथा काली देवी कल्याणमयी भी है।

(6) जो जातक इस साधना को संपूर्ण श्रद्धा व भक्तिभाव पूर्वक करता है वह निश्चित ही चारों वर्गों में स्वामित्व की प्राप्ति करता है व माँ का सामीप्य भी प्राप्त करता है।

(7) साधक को माँ काली असीम आशीष के अतिरिक्त, श्री सुख-सम्पन्नता, वैभव व श्रेष्ठता का भी वरदान प्रदान करती है। साधक का घर कुबेरसंज्ञत अक्षय भंडार बन जाता है।

Benefits from Performing Mahakali Sadhana

The following benefits the aspirant gets automatically by performing the Mahakali Sadhana:

(1) Like all fire-flies get destroyed as they touch the flame of fire, so do all the vices, infatuations and passions of the aspirant as he comes in the contact of Mahakali.

(2) The aspirant who is able to chant the Mahakali Strotra and Mantra has his voice becoming more powerful and influential. His comprehensive power also gets honed up to have an uncanny control over language whether used in poetry or prose.

(3) After Mahakali Sadhana the aspirant has his personality becoming quite imposing and impressive. Such a person has his rivals surrendering even without any confrontation.

(4) He who has mastered Kali Sadhana receives all the special powers and adeptness (Siddhis) naturally and without any effort.

(5) Mother Kali shows her great affection on her devotees. Mother Goddess also ensures their welfare as well.

(6) The aspirant who performs Kali Sadhana with full faith and devotion becomes the leader of all the four castes and feels the presence of the Mother for ever.

(7) The aspirant of this Sadhana becomes capable of influencing every circle he or she moves in. Such a person develops a kind of hypnotic power.

(8) Mother Goddess Kali liberally rewards her devotee or aspirant who performs this Sadhana. Such a person becomes endowed with all the riches, affluence and excellence. His or her coffer never gets emptied like that of the custodian of the divine

(8) काली का उपासक समस्त रोगादि विकारों से अल्पायु आदि से मुक्त हो कर स्वस्थ दीर्घायु जीवन व्यतीत करता है।

(9) काली अपने उपासक को चारों दुर्लभ पुरुषार्थ, महापाप को नष्ट करने की शक्ति, सनातन धर्मी व समस्त भोग प्रदान करती है।

समस्त सिद्धियों की प्राप्ति हेतु सर्वप्रथम गुरु द्वारा दीक्षा अवश्य प्राप्त करें, चूंकि अनंतकाल से गुरु ही सही दिशा दिखाता है एवं शास्त्रों में भी गुरु का एक विशेष स्थान है।

wealth, Kubera.

(9) The aspirant who performs this Sadhana remains free of diseases by the grace of Mother Kali. Such persons never die untimely death.

(10) Mother Kali makes her devotees receive all the four gifts (Dharma, Artha, Kaam, Moksha) of human life effortlessly, destroys even their greatest sins and allows them to enjoy the best things aplenty.

In order to receive all the Siddhis, it is mandatory to first get the initiation by your Guru. It is only the Guru who meticulously picks up the thorns that lie on his disciples' path in the form of pitfalls or mistakes. That is the reason why the scriptures place the Guru on a very high pedestal.

❑❑❑

श्रीमहाकाली पाठ-पूजन विधि

सबसे पहले गणपति का ध्यान करते हुए समस्त देवी-देवताओं को नमस्कार करें।

1. **श्री मन्महागणाधिपतये नमः॥**
   अर्थात्-बुद्धि के देवता श्री गणेश को हमारा नमस्कार है।
2. **लक्ष्मीनारायणाभ्यां नमः॥**
   अर्थात्-सृष्टि के अस्तित्व व अनुभवकर्ता श्री लक्ष्मी व नारायण को हमारा शत-शत नमस्कार है।
3. **उमामहेश्वराभ्यां नमः॥**
   अर्थात्-श्री महादेव व माँ पार्वती को हमारा नमस्कार है।
4. **वाणीहिरण्यगर्भाभ्यां नमः॥**
   अर्थात्-वाणी और उत्पत्ति के कारक माँ सरस्वती व परम ब्रह्मा तुम्हें सादर नमस्कार है।
5. **शचीपुरन्दराभ्यां नमः॥**
   अर्थात्-देवराज इन्द्र व उनकी भार्या शची देवी को हमारा नमस्कार है।
6. **मातृपितृ चरणकमलेभ्यो नमः॥**
   अर्थात्-माता और पिता को हमारा सादर नमस्कार है।
7. **इष्टदेवताभ्यो नमः॥**
   अर्थात्-मेरे इष्ट देवता को मेरा सादर नमस्कार है।
8. **कुलदेवताभ्यो नमः॥**
   अर्थात्-हमारे कुल (खानदान) के देवता तुम्हें नमस्कार है।
9. **ग्रामदेवताभ्यो नमः॥**
   अर्थात्-जिस नगर (ग्राम) से मेरा संबंध है उस स्थान के देवता तुम्हें नमस्कार है।
10. **वास्तुदेवताभ्यो नमः॥**
    अर्थात्-हे वास्तु पुरुष देवता तुम्हें नमस्कार है।

Correct Way to Worship (Read) Mahakali Text (Paath-Poojan)

First of all, mentally invoke Ganapati and bow to all the gods and goddesses.

1. Shree Manmahaganpataye Namah!!

We bow to Lord Ganapati, the deity of wisdom.

2. Lakshmi narayanabhyam Namah!!

Our hundred obeisance to the sustainer and nourisher of the universe Lord Narayana and Goddess Lakshmi.

3. Umamaheshwarabhyam namah!!

We bow to Lord Mahadeva and Mother Parvati.

4. Vaani hiranyagarbhabhyam namah!!

We bow to Goddess of speech Saraswati and the Creator Lord Brahma.

5. Shachee purandarabhyam namah!!

We bow to the Lord of the gods, Indra and his wife Shachee Devi.

6. Matapitribhyam namah!!

We bow to our father and mother.

7. Ishtadevataabhyo namah!!

My respectful homage to my chosen Lord.

8. Kuladevatabhyo namah!!

We bow to our family deity.

9. Gramdevatabhyo namah!!

We bow to our village (or the place of dwelling) deity.

10. Vaastudevatabhyo namah!!

We bow to the Vaastu-Purush deity.

11. Sthaandevatabhyo namah!!

We bow to the deity of this place.

12. Sarvebhyo devebhyo namah!!

We bow to all the gods.

13. Sarvebhyo brahmanebhyo namah!!

Our respectful obeisance to all who are conscious of

11. स्थानदेवताभ्यो नमः॥

अर्थात्-इस स्थान के देवता को सादर नमस्कार है।

12. सर्वेभ्यो देवेभ्यो नमः॥

अर्थात्-समस्त देवताओं को मेरा नमस्कार है।

13. सर्वेभ्यो ब्राह्मणेभ्यो नमः॥

अर्थात्-उन सभी को जिन्हें ब्रह्म का ज्ञान है, मेरा सादर नमस्कार है।

ऊँ भूर्भुवः स्वः।

तत् सवितुर्वरेण्यम्॥ भर्गो देवस्य धीमहि।

धियो यो नः प्रचोदयात्॥

अर्थात्-वह जो असीम परिकल्पना के पार हैं, जिनकी देह सकल, कुशाग्र व कारणात्मक है, हम उस ज्ञान के प्रकाश का ध्यान करते हैं जो समस्त देवों में सर्वोच्च स्थान प्राप्त किए हुए है। हे प्रभु ! हमारे ध्यान में व चिन्तन में तुम सदैव व्याप्त हो।

ऊँ भूः अर्थात् सकल देवी को नमन

ऊँ भुवः अर्थात् कुशाग्र देवी को नमन

ऊँ स्वः अर्थात् कारणात्मक देवी को नमन

ऊँ महः अर्थात् जिसे अस्तित्व का स्वामीत्व प्राप्त है उसे नमस्कार है।

ऊँ जनः अर्थात् ज्ञान की देवी को नमस्कार

ऊँ तपः अर्थात् प्रकाश की देवी को नमस्कार

ऊँ सत्यम् अर्थात् सत्य की देवी को नमस्कार

एते गन्धपुष्पे- पुष्प अर्पण करते समय निम्न मंत्रों का उच्चारण करें-

ऊँ गं गणपतये नमः।

अर्थात्- इन पुष्पों व विशिष्ट गंधों को समर्पित करते हुए गणों के ईश अर्थात् श्री गणेश को ज्ञान का प्रकाश है व बहुसंयोजक है, उन्हें हमारा नमस्कार है।

ऊँ आदित्यादिनवग्रहेभ्यो नमः॥

अर्थात्- इन सुगंधित पुष्पों को समर्पित करते हुए सूर्य सहित नवग्रहों को नमस्कार है।

ऊँ शिवादिपंचदेवताभ्यो नमः॥

अर्थात्- इन सुगंधित पुष्पों को समर्पित करते हुए महादेव सहित पंच देवताओं क्रमशः शिव, शक्ति, विष्णु, गणेश व सूर्य को नमस्कार है।

Brahm (Supreme Spirit).

Aum Bhoobhuvah Svah

Tat Saviturvarenyam!! Bhargo Devasya Dheemahi Dhiyo Yonah Prachodyaat!!

(Meaning that) Who is beyond all imagination, whose body is entirely causative and penetrating—we concentrate our mind on that body of light which rises highest among the gods. O Lord! Be always instinct in our thoughts and mentation.

Aum Bhooh meaning bowing to Sakal Devi.

Aum Bhuvah meaning bowing to Kushagra Devi.

Aum Swah meaning bowing to Kaaranatmaka Devi.

Aum Mahh meaning bowing to that, who is master of all existences.

Aum Janah meaning bowing to the Goddess of Knowledge.

Aum Tapah meaning bowing to the Goddess of Light.

Aum Satyam meaning bowing to the Goddess of Truth.

Ete Grandhapushpe....while offering flowers chant the following mantras:

Aum Gan Ganapataye Namah!

We offer these flowers with distinct smell to Lord Ganesh who spreads the light of knowledge and is a great convenor. We bow to him.

Aum Aadityadinavagrahebhyo Namah!

We bow to the nine planets including the sun while offering these fragrant flowers.

Aum Shivaadipanchadevatabhyo Namah!!

We offer these fragrant flowers to the Five Deities: Shiv, Shakti, Vishnu, Ganesh and the Sun and bow to them in reverence.

Aum Indradidashadikpaalebhyo Namah!!

We offer these fragrant flowers to chief of the gods Indra and the ten guardians of the quarters (Dikapaal) and offer our obeisance.

Aum Matsyaadidashavatarebhyo Namah!!

We offer these fragrant flowers and our obeisance to the super Lord Vishnu who has incarnated ten times as the Fish and other beings.

Aum Prajapataye Namah!!

We offer these fragrant flowers and our obeisance to Prajapita, the creator of this creation.

ॐ इन्द्रादिदशदिक्पालेभ्यो नमः॥

अर्थात्- इन सुगंधित पुष्पों को समर्पित करते हुए देवराज इन्द्र सहित दसों दिशाओं के रक्षकों को नमस्कार है।

ॐ मत्स्यादिदशावतारेभ्यो नमः॥

अर्थात्- इन सुगंधित पुष्पों को समर्पित करते हुए उन परम विष्णु को नमस्कार है, जिन्होंने मत्स्य सहित दस अवतार धारण किए थे।

ॐ प्रजापतये नमः॥

अर्थात्-इन सुगंधित पुष्पों द्वारा सृष्टि के रचयिता को नमस्कार है।

ॐ नमो नारायणाय नमः॥

अर्थात्-इन सुगंधित पुष्पों द्वारा संपूर्ण ज्ञान की चेतना को नमस्कार है।

ॐ सर्वेभ्यो देवेभ्यो नमः॥

अर्थात्-इन सुगंधित पुष्पों द्वारा समस्त देवों को नमस्कार है।

ॐ श्री गुरवे नमः॥

अर्थात्-इन सुगंधित पुष्पों द्वारा गुरु को नमस्कार है।

ॐ ब्राह्मणेभ्यो नमः॥

अर्थात्- इन सुगंधित पुष्पों द्वारा ज्ञान के समस्त परिचितों (ब्राह्मणों) को सादर नमस्कार है।

निम्न मंत्र का उच्चारण करते हुए दाहिने हाथ की मध्यमा में या कलाई पर घास को बांधें-

ॐ कुशासने स्थितो ब्रह्मा कुशे चैव जनार्दनः।
कुशे ह्याकाशवद् विष्णुः कुशासन नमोऽस्तुते॥

अर्थात्- इस कुश (घास) में परम ब्रह्म का प्रकाश स्थित है तथा इसी में निवास करते हैं श्री जनार्दन भी। इसी कुश के प्रकाश में स्वयं परम विष्णु का प्रकाश भी विद्यमान है, अतः मैं इस कुश के आसन को नमस्कार करता हूं।

आचमन करते समय निम्न मंत्रों का उच्चारण करें-

ॐ केशवाय नमः।

अर्थात्-विष्णुरूप केशव को नमस्कार है।

ॐ माधवाय नमः।

अर्थात्-श्री विष्णु रूप माधव को नमस्कार है।

ॐ गोविन्दाय नमः।

अर्थात्-श्री विष्णु रूप गोविन्दा प्रभु को नमस्कार है।

Aum Namo Narayanay Namah!!

We bow to the awareness of the entire knowledge through these fragrant flowers.

Aum Sarvebhyo Devebhyo Namah!

We pay obeisance to all the gods through the offering of these fragrant flowers.

Aum Shree Guruve Namah!!

We offer our obeisance to our Guru through these flowers.

Aum Bramanebhyo Namah!

We obeisance the Brahmanas, well aware of all knowledge through these fragrant flowers.

While chanting the following mantra tie a blade of grass on the right hand's middle finger or on the wrist:

Aum Kushasane Sthito Brahma Kushe Cheiva Janardanah
Kushe Hayakaashvad Vishnuh Kushasan Namostute!!

Reposed in the Kusha (grass) is the light of the Supreme Being and Janardan also dwells in it. Param Vishnu's light is also present in this Kusha so I bow to this Kusha-asana (Kusha-seat).

While raising your hands with water chant the following mantras:

Aum Keshavaaya Namah!

I bow to Keshava in the form of Lord Vishnu.

Aum Maadhavaya Namah!

I bow to Maadhava form of Lord Vishnu!

Aum Govindaaya Namah!

I bow to Govinda form of Lord Vishnu!

Aum Vishnuh Aum Vishnuh Aum Vishnuh!
Aum Heem Shreem Kreem Parmeshwari Kaalike Namah.

Water Purification

At the place of *Pooja*, prepare the following '*yantra*' with the help of sandalwood water solution in a *Thaali* (edged plate). Now while chanting the following four mantras, sprinkle the *Akshata* (rice) grain on to the *Thaali* (Yantra):

(1) Aum Aadhaarshaktye Namah!

We bow to the base of our strength.

(2) Aum Kummarya Namah !!

We bow to Him who supports the earth and nourishes the creation.

ऊँ विष्णुः ऊँ विष्णुः ऊँ विष्णुः॥

ऊँ ह्रीं श्रीं क्रीं परमेश्वरि कालिके नमः।

जल शुद्धि

जल की शुद्धि हेतु सर्वप्रथम चित्रानुसार यंत्र एक थाली अथवा पूजन स्थान पर चंदन व पानी मिलाकर बनाए घोल से तैयार करें। अब निम्न चारों मंत्रों के साथ यंत्र पर अक्षत (चावल) अर्पण करें-

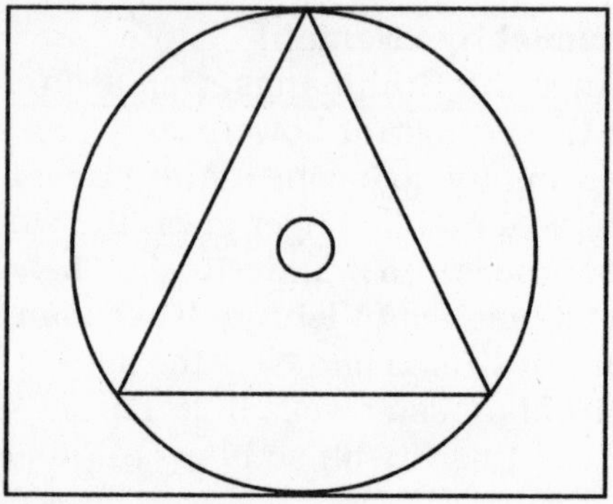

(1) ऊँ आधारशक्तये नमः।

अर्थात्-शक्ति के आधार को नमस्कार है।

(2) ऊँ कुर्म्मायै नमः॥

अर्थात्- पृथ्वी को जो समर्थन देता है व सृष्टि का भरण-पोषण करता है उसे नमस्कार है।

(3) ऊँ अनन्ताय नमः॥

अर्थात्- जो अनन्त है उसे नमस्कार है।

(4) ऊँ पृथिव्यै नमः॥

अर्थात्-माँ पृथ्वी को नमस्कार है।

निम्न मंत्र का उच्चारण करते समय फट बोलने के साथ एक खाली पात्र को केन्द्र में दर्शाये बिंदु पर रखें।

ॐ स्थां स्थीं स्थिरो भव फट्।

जो सकल शरीर में स्थित है, कुशाग्र देह में स्थित है व कारणात्मक में भी स्थित है, वे शुद्धि करें।

अब इस खाली पात्र में गंगाजल डालते समय निम्न मंत्र का उच्चारण करें-

ऊँ गंगे च यमुने चैव गोदावरि सरस्वती।

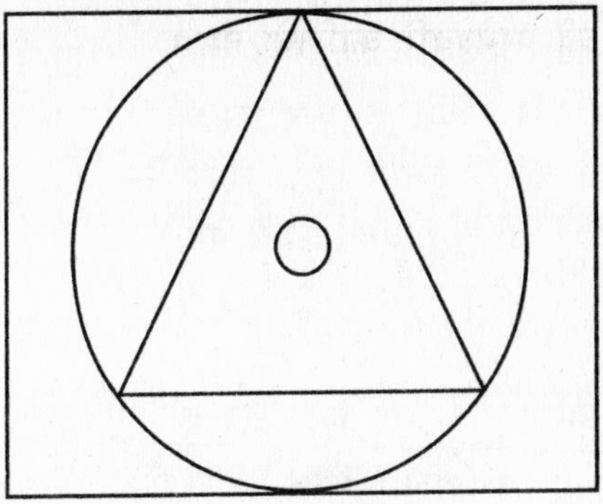

(3) Aum Anantaay Namah!!

We bow to Him who is Infinite.

(4) Aum Prithvyei Namah!!

We bow to the mother earth.

Now while chanting the following mantra, make sure that when you say '*Phut*' keep an empty vessel at the central point as shown in the figure:

Aum Stham Stheem Sthiro Bhav Phut!!

May he who is reposed in the '*sakal*' body, in the *Kushagra* '*Deh*' and also in the *Kaaranatmak*, purify us.

Now while putting some *Ganga jala* in the empty vessel, chant the following mantra:

Aum Gange Cha Jamune Cheiva Godavari Saraswati!
Narmade Sindhu Kaveri Jalasmin Sannidhim Kuru!!

Meaning, I collect the waters of the seven rivers—Ganga, Jamuna, Godavari, Saraswati, Narmada, Sindhu and Kaveri— in this vessel.

Then after, while putting the leaves of *Tulsi* chant the following *mantra*:

Aum En Heem Kleem Shree Vrindavana vaa Sinje Namah!

Meaning, we bow to Tulsi Goddess who dwells in Vrindavan and who makes one learned, wise and rich.

Now, while chanting the following mantras put three flowers in the water:

Etey Gandhapushpe Aum Aum Arkamandalaaya Dwaadash Kalaatmne Namah!

While offering these fragrant flowers I bow reverentially to the twelve forms of the Sun: Tapini, Taapini, Dhoomra,

नर्मदे सिन्धु कावेरि जलेऽस्मिन् सन्निधिं कुरु॥

अर्थात्- मैं सातों नदियों क्रमशः गंगा, जमुना, गोदावरी, सरस्वती, नर्मदा, सिन्धु व कावेरी का जल इस एक पात्र में एकत्रित करता हूं।

इसके पश्चात् जल में तुलसी डालते समय निम्न मंत्र का उच्चारण करें-

ऊँ ऐं ह्रीं क्लीं श्रीं वृन्दावनवासिन्यै नमः।

अर्थात्- ऊँ ज्ञान, धन, बुद्धि व वृन्दावन में वास करने वाली देवी तुलसी को मेरा सादर नमस्कार है।

अब निम्न मंत्रों का उच्चारण करते हुए तीन पुष्प जल में डालें-

एते गन्धपुष्पे ऊँ अं अर्कमंडलाय द्वादशकलात्मने नमः।

अर्थात्- इन सुगंधित पुष्पों को समर्पित करते हुए मैं सूर्य के द्वादश (बारह) आकारों क्रमशः तपिनी, तापिनी, धूम्रा, मरीचि, ज्वालिनी, रुचि, सुधूम्रा, भूः गदा, विश्वा, बोधिनी, धारिणी व सूक्ष्मा को सादर नमस्कार है।

एते गन्धपुष्पे ऊँ उं सोममंडलाय षोडशकलात्मने नमः।

अर्थात्- इन सुगंधित पुष्पों को समर्पित करते हुए मैं चन्द्रमा की सोलह कलाओं क्रमशः अमृता, प्राणदा, पूषा, तुश्ती, पुश्ती, रति, धृति, शशिनी, चंद्रिका, कांति, ज्योत्स्ना, श्री, प्रीति, अंगदा, पूर्णा, पूर्णमृता को सादर नमस्कार है।

एते गन्धपुष्पे ऊँ मं वह्निमंडलाय दशकलात्मने नमः।

अर्थात्- इन सुगंधित पुष्पों को समर्पित करते हुए मैं अग्नि की दसों कलाओं क्रमशः धूम्रा, अर्चित, ज्वलिनी, सूक्ष्मा, ज्वालिनी, विषफुलिंगीनी, सुश्री, सुरूपा, कपिला व हव्यकव्यवहा को सादर नमस्कार है।

तत्पश्चात् दोनों हाथों को जोड़कर निम्न मंत्र का उच्चारण करें-

ऊँ ह्रीं श्रीं क्रीं परमेश्वरि कालिके नमः।

अर्थात्- धन, वृद्धि, विघटन की परम शक्ति माँ काली मैं अपने आपको समर्पित करते हुए तुम्हें नमस्कार करता हूं।

अब सभी वस्तुओं तथा स्वयं पर निम्न मंत्र का उच्चारण करते हुए जल छिड़कें-

अमृताम् कुरु नमः।

*अर्थात्-*हे देवि! इस जल को अमृत बना दो। तुम्हें नमस्कार है।

Marichi, Jwaalini, Ruchi, Sudhoomra, Bhubgada, Vishwa, Bodhini, Dharini and Kshaamaa.

Etey Gandhapushpe Aum Aum Somamandalaay Shodasha Kalaatmane Namah!

(Meaning) While offering these fragrant flowers, I bow reverentially to the sixteen phases of the Moon: Amrita, Pranada, Poosha, Tushtee, Pusti, Rati, Dhriti, Shashani, Chandrika, Kaanti, Jyotsana, Shree, Preeti, Angadaa, Poorna, Poornamrita.

Etey Gandhapushpe Aum Man Vahirmandalaay Dashkalatmane Namah!

While offering these fragrant flowers, I bow reverentially to the ten phases of Agni: Dhoomna, Archita, Jwalini, Sookshma, Jwaalini, Vishphullangini, Sushree, Suroopa, Kapila and Havyakavyavaha.

Now put both the hands together and chant the following Mantra:

Aum Hreen Shreen Kreen Parmeshwari Kaalike Namah!

I totally surrender myself to the shelter of Mother Kali and bow to her who is the ultimate repository of all wealth, growth and dissipation.

Now sprinkle some water over yourself and all the objects thus far used while chanting the following mantra:

Amritaam Kuru Namah!

(Meaning): O Goddess convert this water into nectar. I bow to you.

Flower Purification

Chant the following mantra for flower purification (or purification through the flowers):

Aum Pushpa Pushpa Mahapushpa Supushpa Pushp Sambhave!

Pushpa Chayaavakeerne Cha Hum Phut Namah!!

Meaning, O flowers, great and best flowers, the mounds of flowers, the flowers that lie scattered, eliminate your identity to purify the ambience. My obeisance to them.

पुष्प शुद्धि-

फूलों की शुद्धि हेतु निम्न मंत्र का उच्चारण करें-

ऊँ पुष्प पुष्प महापुष्प सुपुष्प पुष्पसम्भवे।
पुष्पचयावकीर्णे च हुं फट् नमः॥

अर्थात्-हे पुष्पों-पुष्पों, महान पुष्पों, उत्तम पुष्पों, पुष्पों के ढेर व जो बिखरे हुए पुष्प हैं उनके अहं को समाप्त कर उनकी शुद्धि करें।

उन पुष्पों को नमस्कार है।

काली गायत्री

ऊँ महाकाल्यै च विद्महे श्मशानवासिन्यै च धीमहि।
तन्नो काली प्रचोदयात्॥

अर्थात्- हम उस महाशक्ति का ध्यान करते हैं जो अंधेरों को दूर करती है। हम उनका चिन्तन करते हैं, जिनका निवास स्थल श्मशान भूमि है। वह महामयी महाकाली हमें समृद्धि व उन्नति प्रदान करें।

श्रीमहाकाली का ध्यान-

करालवदनां घोरां मुक्तकेशी चतुर्भुजाम्।
कालिकां दक्षिणां दिव्यां मुण्डमालाविभूषितम्॥

सद्यश्छिन्नशिरः खड्गवामाधोर्ध्वकराम्भुजाम्।
अभयां वरदाञ्चैव दक्षिणोर्ध्वाधः पाणिकाम्॥

महामेघप्रभां श्यामां तथा चैव दिगम्बरीम्।
कण्ठावस्क्तमुण्डालीगलद्रुधिरचर्चिचताम्॥

कर्णावतंसतानीतशव युग्मभयानकम्।
घोरदंष्ट्रां करालास्यां पीनोन्नतपयोधराम॥

शवानां करसंघातैः कृतकाञ्ची हसन्मुखीम्।
सृक्कद्वय-गलद्रक्तधारा-विस्पुरिताननाम्॥

Kali Gayatri

Aum Mahakaalpei Cha Vidmahe Smashaan Vasinye Cha Dheemahi!

Tanno Kali Prachodyaat!!

Meaning, we concentrate our Dhyan on that Great Power that eliminates darkness, we think of Her whose dwelling place is crematorium. May that Grand Mahakali provide us prosperity and progress.

The Dhyan (concentrating on) Of Shree Mahakali

Karalavadanam Ghorah Muktakeshi Chaturbhuja!
Kaalikam Dakshina Divyam Mundamala Vibhushitam!!

Sadyash Chhinnashirah Khangavamordhva Karaam Bhujam!
Abhayam Varadaancheiva Dakhishordhardham Paanikam!!

Maha Megha Prabham Shyaamam Tatha Cheiva Digambarim!
Kantha va Rakta Mundaalee Galadrudhir Charchitam!!

Karnavatanstaa Neeta Shava Yogma Bhayanakam!
Ghorandrashtram Karaalaasyam Peendtata Payodharam!!

Shavanam Kara Sangha Teith Kritamkaanchee Hasanmvheem!
Sukkadvaya Galad rakta Dhaara Vispuritaannaam!!

Ghoraraavaam Maharaudraeem Smashaanaalayavaasineem!
Balaark Amandalaakaarlo Chan Trita Tayaanvitam!!

Dan Turam Dakshin Vyaapi Muktaalanvika Chochchyam!
Shava Roopa Mahadevahridayoparisansthitan!!

Shiva Bhiryoranravaa Bhi Shchaturchhikhu Samanvitam!
Mahakaalen Cha Samam Vipareejartaa Turam!!

Sukh Prasanna Vadanam Smeraanan saroruham!
Evam Sanchi Yantayet Kaaleem Sarvakaam Samriddhdaam!!

Aum Kreem Kreem Kreem Hum Hum Hreem Hreem Dakshine Kalike Kreem Kreem Kreem Hum Hum Hreem Hreem Swaahaa!

(Meaning)

Devi Mahakali's voice is terribly frightening. Her hair is spread all around, she has four arms and her neck is adorned with garland of hacked heads. Her lower left hand carries a recently hacked off head and the upper right hand a sword.

घोररावां महारौद्रीं श्मशानालयवासिनीम्।
बालार्कमण्डलाकारलोचनत्रितयान्विताम्।।

दन्तुरां दक्षिणव्यापि मुक्तालन्विकचोच्चयाम्।
शवरूप महादेवहृदयोपरिसंस्थिताम्।।
शिवाभिर्घोररवाभिश्चतुर्दिक्षु समन्विताम्।
महाकालेन च समं विपरीतरतातुराम्।।

सुखं प्रसन्नवदनां स्मेराननसरोरुहाम्।
एवं संचिन्तयेत् कालीं सर्वकामसमृद्धिदाम्।।

ऊँ क्रीं क्रीं हुं हुं ह्रीं ह्रीं दक्षिणे कालिके क्रीं क्रीं हुं हुं ह्रीं ह्रीं स्वाहा।

अर्थात्- देवी महाकाली का स्वर अत्यंत भयंकर है। उनके बाल बिखरे हुए हैं, चार भुजाएं हैं व गले में जिनके मुंडमाला विभूषित है। उनके निचले वाम हस्त (बाएं हाथ) में अभिनव कटा हुआ मुंड है व ऊपर वाले बाहिने हाथ में खड्ग धारण किए हुए है। निचले दाहिने हाथ से वह अभयदान देती हैं वह ऊपर वाले दाहिने हाथ से वह आशीर्वाद प्रदान करती हैं। वह किसी गहरे काले बादल जैसी चमकती हैं व निर्वस्त्र हैं। उनके कंठ में जो मुंडमाला झूल रही है उसके बहते हुए रक्त से पूरा शरीर भीग गया है। उनके दोनों कानों में कुंडल की भांति दो शिशुओं के शव सुशोभित हैं एवं इसी कारणवश उनकी आकृति अत्यंत भयावह दृष्ट होती है। उनके बहिक्षेप्य दो दांत अत्यंत ही भयानक दिखाई पड़ते हैं व उनके दानों स्तनों से लगातार दुग्ध की धार बह रही है। वह कमरबंध के स्थान पर अपनी कटि में शवों के हाथों से निर्मित करधनी धारण किए हुए हैं। इन मुख पर एक दिव्य मुस्कान है। रक्तपान के पश्चात् उनके कपोलों के दोनों किनारों से जो रक्त बह रहा है वह किसी नदी के समान प्रतीत होता है।

अत्यंत भयानक व घोर क्रोधावेश में अति गंभीर शब्दों का उच्चारण करती है। उनका निवास स्थान शमशान है। उनके तीनों नेत्र क्रमशः अग्नि, सूर्य व चन्द्रमा हैं। उन्होंने अपने हाथ में तपस्वियों का कमंडल धारण किया हुआ है। दक्षिण व्यापी होते हुए भी वह सभी जगह विद्यमान हैं, फिर भी सबसे असम्बद्ध हैं। वह अत्यंत ही सहजतापूर्वक शव रूपी शिव के हृदय पर अवस्थित हैं। देवी की शक्तियां (शिवाएं) चारों दिशाओं में भयंकर अट्टहास का उत्सर्जन करती घूम रही हैं। एवं देवी महाकाल के साथ विपरीत भाव में आनन्दित दिखाई देती हैं।

With her lower right hand she offers assurance (Swasti) to all and with her upper right hand she blesses all. She is unclad and shines like a deep dense cloud. The blood from the garland of the hacked heads has drenched her body totally. Her two ears are adorned with the two dead bodies of the infants which appear like her earrings. Owing to her this decor, she appears extremely frightening. Her two protruding teeth add to her frightening visage and her two breasts constantly ooze out milk. Her waist is girdled by the chain of the hacked heads from the corpses. Her visage shows a divine smile. The blood that spills out of her lips when she drinks blood appears to run like a bloodied stream of river.

She utters most horrendous words in her extreme rage which is truly frightening. Her dwelling place is the crematorium. Her three eyes are fire, the moon and the sun. She carries a 'Kamandal' (water pot) like the one carried by the ascetics. Despite being south pervading, she permeates all directions but still totally unattached with anyone in particular. Very naturally she reposes like a dead body over the heart of Lord Shiv. Her powers (Shivaayen) are moving about in every direction letting out mafficking laughters. But the Goddess when with Mahakaal (Time) appears blissful in totally opposite feeling.

She thus usurps all darkness. She is the fulfiller of all desires (of the aspirants on her devotees) and all should concentrate their mind on that Goddess Mahakaali with the following request:

"O Goddess! Like you had humbled the pride of all the demons, you should also eliminate the arrogance which rises in my mind like a demon to redeem me from their influence and provide all peace and prosperity to me. I surrender myself before you and offer my obeisance to you."

While offering the Naivedya (oblations) the following mantras should be chanted:

Aagachchheha Mahadevi! Sarva Sam Pata Pradaayini!

Yaavat Vratam Samaapyet Taaktvam Sannidhau Bhava!!

Aum Hreelm Shreem Kreem Parameshwari Kaalike Namah Aavaahnam Samarpayaami!

(Meaning) 'O Mahadevi! You are the bestower of all happiness. Please come here and remain seated here till this

इस प्रकार समस्त अंधेरों का हरण व वरदान स्वरूप मनोकामनाओं की पूर्ति करने वाली देवि महाकाली का ध्यान अवश्य करना चाहिए।

"हे देवि! जिस प्रकार तुमने दैत्यों के अहं को नष्ट किया उसी प्रकार मेरे अंदर अहं रूपी जो दानव विद्यमान है उसका संहार कर मेरे समस्त कष्टों से मेरा निवारण कर मुझे सुख व समृद्धि प्रदान करो। मैं स्वयं को तुम पर समर्पित कर तुम्हें नमस्कार करता हूं।"

देवि को नैवेद्य अर्पित करते समय निम्न मंत्र का उच्चारण करें–

आगच्छेह महादेवि ! सर्वसम्पत्प्रदायिनि।
यावद् व्रतं समाप्येत तावत्त्वं सन्निधौ भव॥
ऊँ ह्रीं श्रीं क्रीं परमेश्वरि कालिके नमः आवाहनं समर्पयामि।

अर्थात्–हे महादेवि! सभी सुखों की दात्री, कृपया पधारिए व जब तक यह पूजन समाप्त नहीं होता यहीं विराजमान रहें। मेरे इस आमंत्रण पर हे समृद्धि, वृद्धि व विघटन की महादेवि, तुम आओ! मैं स्वयं को तुम्हें समर्पित करते हुए तुम्हारा आवाहन करता हूं।

आसन हेतु निम्न मंत्र का उच्चारण करें–

अनेकरत्नसंयुक्तं नानामणिगणान्वितम्।
कार्तस्वरमयं दिव्यमासनं प्रतिगृह्यताम्॥
ऊँ ह्रीं श्रीं क्रीं परमेश्वरि कालिके नमः आसनं समर्पयामि

अर्थात्–अनेक रत्नों व बहुमूल्य मणियों से जड़ित यह आसन देवि स्वेच्छा से कृपया ग्रहण करें। इस आसन के आमंत्रण सहित हे समृद्धि, वृद्धि व विघटन की महादेवि! मैं स्वयं को भी तुमको समर्पित करता हूं, मुझे स्वीकार करो।

देविचरणों के स्नान हेतु निम्न मंत्र का उच्चारण करें–

ऊँ गंगादिसर्वतीर्थेभ्यो मया प्रार्थनयाहृतम्।
तोयमेतत् सुखस्पर्शं पाद्यार्थं प्रतिगुह्यताम्॥
ऊँ ह्रीं श्रीं क्रीं परमेश्वरि कालिके नमः पाद्यं समर्पयामि।

अर्थात्–गंगा सति समस्त तीर्थों से लाए गए जलों को मिश्रित कर इस पूजा में लाया गया है। मैं इस जल को आपके चरणों में अर्पण करता हूं, कृपया अपने कमलरूपी चरणों द्वारा इसे छूकर स्वीकार करें। हे समृद्धि, वृद्धि व विघटन की महादेवि मैं स्वयं को इस चरणामृत के साथ तुम्हें समर्पित करता हूं, मुझे स्वीकार करो।

देवि के हाथों व मुंह को प्रक्षालित करने हेतु निम्न मंत्र का उच्चारण करें–

कर्पूरेण सुगन्धेन सुरभिस्वादु शीतलम्।

entire worship is over. At my this invocation, O Goddess of all decay and growth and prosperity, you must come here. I totally surrender myself unto you and invoke you here."

Before offering her the assigned seat, chant the following mantra:

Anekaratnasamyutam Nanamanigandaan Vitam!
Kaarta Swaramayam Divya Masanam Pratigrihyataam!!
Aum Hreem Shreem Kreem Parameshwari Kalike Namah Aasana Samarpayaami!

(Meaning) May the Goddess voluntarily occupy this seat embedded with many gems and precious jewels. Along with this invitation to you to occupy the seat, I surrender myself unto you and invoke you, the Goddess of all growth, decay and prosperity. Please accept me!

Before bathing the feet of the Goddess, the following mantra should be chanted:

Aum Gangaadi Sarvateethebhyo Maya Prarthanaahritam!
Toyametat Sukhsparsham Padyaartham Pratighyataam!!
Aum Hreem Shreem Kreem Parameshwari Kaalike Namah Paadyam Samarpayaam!

(Meaning) The water brought from all the holy Teerthas including that from Ganga have been mixed for the worship here. The same water I offer to your feet. Please touch it with your lotus feet and show your acceptance. O Goddess of all prosperity, growth and decay, I surrender myself unto you with this Charanamrita. Please accept me.

Now, before washing the hands and mouth of the Goddess chant the following mantra:

Karpoorani Sugandhena Surabhiswaad Sheetalam!
Toya Maachamaneeyartham Devidam Pratigrihyataam!!
Aum Hreem Shreem Kreem Parameshwari Kaalike Namah
Aachamaneeyam Samarpayaami!

(Meaning) Fragranted with camphor and other perfumes, I offer you this water, extremely cool and very tasty. O Goddess, please accept it. O Goddess of all growth, decay and prosperity, with the offering of this water for the rinsing purpose, I surrender myself unto you. Please accept me as

तोयमाचमनीयार्थं देवीदं प्रतिगृह्यताम्॥

ऊँ ह्रीं श्रीं क्रीं परमेश्वरि कालिके नमः आचमनीयं समर्पयामि।

अर्थात्-कपूर व अन्य सुगंधों सहित, अतिशीतल व श्रेष्ठ स्वाद से भरपूर, इस जल को मैं तुम्हें अर्पण करता हूं, हे देवि इसे स्वीकार करो। इस आचमन के अर्पण सहित हे समृद्धि, वृद्धि व विघटन की महादेवि! मैं स्वयं को भी तुमको समर्पित करता हूं। कृपया मुझे स्वीकार करो।

देवि के अहर्य हेतु निम्न मंत्र का उच्चारण करें-

निधीनां सर्वदेवानां त्वमनर्घ्यगुणा ह्यसि।

सिंहोपरिस्थिते देवि! गृहाणार्घ्यं नमोऽस्तु ते॥

ऊँ ह्रीं श्रीं क्रीं परमेश्वरि कालिके नमः अर्घ्यं समर्पयामि।

अर्थात्-समस्त देवी-देवताओं को तुम्हें समर्पित करने पर, हे अर्घ्य! तुम स्नेह बाहुल्य सुख प्रदान करना। हे सिंह पर स्थित देवि! इस अर्घ्य को स्वीकार करो। इस अर्घ्य सहित मैं स्वयं को भी तुम्हें समर्पित करता हूं। मुझे स्वीकार करो।

मधुपर्क अर्पित करते समय निम्न मंत्र का उच्चारण करें-

दधिमधुघृतसमायुक्तं पात्रयुग्मं समन्वितम्।

मधुपर्कं गृहाण त्वं शुभदा भव शोभने॥

ऊँ ह्रीं श्रीं क्रीं परमेश्वरि कालिके नमः मधुपर्कं समर्पयामि।

अर्थात्-दही, शहद, घी सभी को साथ एक पात्र में डाल कर बनाए गए इस मधुपर्क को हे देवि! मैं तुम्हें अर्पण करता हूं। यह तुम्हारी कांति को शुद्धता पहुंचाएगा। इस मधुपर्क सहित, हे समृद्धि, वृद्धि व विघटन की महादेवि मैं स्वयं को भी तुम्हें समर्पित करता हूं, मुझे स्वीकार करो।

गंगा स्नान हेतु जल चढ़ाते समय निम्न मंत्र का उच्चारण करें-

ऊँ गंगे च यमुने चैव गोदावरि सरस्वती।

नर्मदे सिन्धु कावेरि स्नानार्थं प्रतिगृह्यताम्॥

ऊँ ह्रीं श्रीं क्रीं परमेश्वरि कालिके नमः गंगास्नानं समर्पयामि।

अर्थात्-देवि! गंगा, जमुना, सरस्वती, गोदावरी, नर्मदा, सिन्धु व कावेरी नदियों से यह जल विशेष रूप से तुम्हारे स्नान हेतु लाया गया है, कृपया इसे स्वीकार करें। इस गंगाजल सहित हे समृद्धि, वृद्धि व विघटन की महादेवि कालिका मैं स्वयं को तुम्हें समर्पित करता हूं, मुझे स्वीकार करो।

कंगन समर्पण हेतु निम्न मंत्र का उच्चारण करें-

ऊँ माणिक्यमुक्ताखंडयुक्ते सुवर्णकारेण च संस्कृते ये।

ते किङ्किणीभिः स्वरिते सुवर्णे मयाऽर्पितो देवि गृहाण कङ्कणे॥

well.

For the Devi's Aharya (oblation etc.) chant this mantra:

Nidheenam Sarvadevaanam Twamanarghyaguna Hayaasi!

Sinho Paristhite Devi Grihaanaharya Namostu Te!!

Aum Hreem Shreem Kreem Parmeshwari Kaalike Namah Aharya Samarpayaami!

O Aharya (oblation etc)! When you are offered to all the gods and goddesses, grant me much of affection and happiness on their behalf. O Goddess seated on the lion, please accept this Aharya (or Arghye). Please accept my surrender also.

When offering Madhuparka, chant the following mantra:

Dadhi Madhughrita Samaayuktam Paatrayugmam Samanvitam!

Madhuparka Grihaan Twam Shubhda Bhava Shobhane!!

Aum Hreem Shreem Kreem Parameshwari Kaalike
Namah Madhuparka Samarpayaami!!

(Meaning), O Goddess! I offer you this Madhuparka (made from mixing curds, ghee, honey, sugar and water) in a pot for your consumption. This shall enhance your glow and piety. I offer you myself along with this Madhuparka—please accept me.

While pouring down Ganga jala for the Goddess's bath, chant the following strotra:

Aum Ganga Cha Jamune Chaiva Godavari Saraswati!

Narmade Sindhu Kaveri Snanahrtha Prat, Grihya Taam!!

Aum Hreem Shreem Kreem Parameshwari Kaalike Namah!!

Gangasnaanam Samarpayaami!

(Meaning), O Goddess, this water collected from Ganga, Yamuna, Saraswati, Godavari, Sindhu, Kaveri rivers for the purpose of your bath, I offer to you. Please accept it. O Goddess of growth, decay and prosperity, I offer myself to your shelter. Please accept me, along with this water.

Before adorning her with the bangle (Kangan), chant the following mantra:

Aum Manikyamuktakhandayukte Suvarnakarena Cha Sanskrite Ye!

ऊँ ह्रीं श्रीं क्रीं परमेश्वरि कालिके नमः कङ्कणं समर्पयामि।

अर्थात्–जो बहुमूल्य रत्नों, माणिक्यों मुक्ता आदि से जड़ित हैं व उत्तम स्वर्ण में बना है एवं संस्कृत के अक्षर जिसमें लिखे हुए हैं, वह कंगन हे देवि! मैं तुम्हें समर्पित करता हूं। इसे स्वीकार करो। इस कंगन सहित हे समृद्धि, वृद्धि व विघटन की महादेवि कालिका मैं स्वयं को तुम्हें समर्पित करता हूं, मुझे स्वीकार करो।

शंखाभूषण अर्पण करते समय निम्न पंत्र का उच्चारण करें–

ऊँ शंखञ्च विविधं चित्रं बाहूनाञ्च विभूषणम्।

मया निवेदितं भक्तया गृहाण परमेश्वरि॥

ऊँ ह्रीं श्रीं क्रीं परमेश्वरि कालिके नमः शङ्खालंकारं समर्पयामि।

अर्थात्–मैं पूर्ण भक्तिभाव से हे देवि! तुम्हें विभिन्न प्रकार के विशिष्ट शंखों द्वारा निर्मित आभूषण समर्पित करता हूं, कृपया इन्हें स्वीकार करो। इन शंखाभूषणों सहित हे देवि! मैं स्वयं को भी तुम्हें समर्पित करता हूं, कृपया मुझे स्वीकार करो।

आभूषण अर्पण हेतु निम्न मंत्र का उच्चारण करें–

ऊँ दिव्यरत्नसमायुक्ता वह्निभानुसमप्रभाः।

गात्राणि शोभयिष्यन्ति अलङ्काराः सुरेश्वरि॥

ऊँ ह्रीं श्रीं क्रीं परमेश्वरि कालिकायै नमः अलङ्कारान् समर्पयामि।

अर्थात्–अग्नि के प्रकाश रूपी दिव्य रत्नों व सूर्य जैसी चमक वाले माणिक्यों से सुशोभित यह आभूषण हे देवि! तुम्हें अर्पित करता हूं, कृपया इन्हें स्वीकार करो। इन आभूषणों सहित समृद्धि, वृद्धि व विघटन की महादेवि! मैं स्वयं को भी तुम्हें समर्पित करता हूं, कृपया मुझे स्वीकार करो।

अक्षत (चावल) चढ़ाते समय निम्न मंत्र का उच्चारण करें–

अक्षतान् निर्मलान् शुद्धान् मुक्ताफलसमन्वितम्।

गृहाणेमान् महोदेवि देहि मे निर्मलां धियम्॥

ऊँ ह्रीं श्रीं क्रीं परमेश्वरि कालिके नमः अक्षतान् समर्पयामि।

अर्थात्–हे देवि! कृपया इन अक्षतों को स्वीकार करो एवं यह शुद्धता, स्वच्छता व मुक्तिफल का प्रतीक है उसी प्रकार हमारे मस्तिष्क की समस्त अशुद्धियों को पूरा कर तुम हमें स्वच्छता व शुद्धता प्रदान करो। इन अक्षतों सहित हे समृद्धि, वृद्धि व विघटन की महादेवि! मैं स्वयं को तुम्हें समर्पित करता हूं, मुझे स्वीकार करो।

Te Kingante Bhih Swarate Suvarne Mayaarpito Devi Grihaani Kankane!!

Aum Hreem Shreem Kreem Parameshwari Kaalike Namah Kankane Samarpayami!

(Meaning) This bangle, embedded with ruby, pearl and other costly gems and made of gold, on which an inscription is made in Sanskrit, I offer to you Devi! Please accept it. I offer this to you, O Goddess of growth, decay and prosperity, along with this gem embedded bangle, my own self. Please accept me as well.

While offering 'Shankhabhushana' (conch-shell and other ornaments), chant the following mantra:

Aum Sankhkanch Vividham Chitram Bahunanch Vibhushanan

Maya Niveditam Bhakataya Grihan Parmeshwari

Aum Hreem Shreem Kreem Parameshwari Kalilikaaya Namah Shankhalakaram

(Meaning), O Goddess with my total being devoted to you I offer you ornaments made from a variety of conch-shells. Please accept them. With these ornaments, O Devi, I offer myself unto your grace. Please accept me as well.

Before offering other decoration, chant the following mantra:

Aum Divyaratnasamaayuktam Vahni Bhanu Samapraphah!

Gaatrani Shobhyishiyanti Alankarah Sureshwari!!

Aum Hreem Shreem Kreem Parameshwari Kaalikaaye

Namah Alankaraan Samarpayaami!

O Goddess, resplendent with the gems and jewels shining as brightly as the sun, I offer these ornaments to you. Please accept them. O Goddess of growth, decay and prosperity. I also, alongwith these ornaments, offer myself to you. Please accept me as well.

While offering the Goddess the food, chant this mantra.

Aum Satpatram Shuddha Suhavi Virvardhaneka Bhakshanam!

Nivedayaami Deveshi Sarva Triptakaram Param!!

Aum Annapoorney Sadaa Poorne Shankar Pravavallabhe

Gyan-Vairagya Siddyartha Bhiksham Dehi Namostute!!

Mata Cha Parvati Devi Pita Devo Maheshwarah!!

देवी को आहार हेतु भोजन अर्पण करते समय निम्न मंत्र का उच्चारण करें-

ऊँ सत्पात्रं शुद्धसुहविर्विधानेकभक्षणम्।
निवेदयामि देवेशि सर्वतृप्तिकरं परम्॥
ऊँ अन्नपूर्णे सदा पूर्णे शङ्करप्राणवल्लभे।
ज्ञानवैराग्यसिद्ध्यर्थं भिक्षां देहि च पार्वती॥
माता च पार्वती देवी पिता देवो महेश्वरः।
बान्धवाः शिवभक्ताश्च स्वदेशो भुवनत्रयम्॥

ऊँ ह्रीं श्रीं क्रीं परमेश्वरि कालिके नमः भोगनैवेद्यम् समर्पयामि।

अर्थात्-इस अतिशुद्ध पात्र में विविध प्रकार का अतिशुद्ध भोजन, जो हे देवि आपको अर्पित किया गया है वह आपको श्रेष्ठतम व उत्तम प्रकार का सन्तोष प्रदान करे। हे अन्न की देवि अन्नपूर्णा! तुम संपूर्ण हो, तुम ही शांतिदूत महाशिव की प्राण शक्ति हो। हे देवी! ज्ञान, लाभ, परित्याग, विवेक एवं पूर्णता का हमें दान दो। हम तुम्हें झुक कर सादर नमस्कार करते हैं। हमारी माता देवी पार्वती व पिता महेश्वर महादेव हैं। त्रिलोकों के अधिपति व अच्छाई व शालीनता की अखंड चेतना श्री महेश्वर महादेव का उनके उपासकों द्वारा आवाहन किया जाता है। इस भोग नैवेद्य के साथ हे समृद्धि! वृद्धि व विघटन की देवि! मैं स्वयं को भी तुम्हें समर्पित करता हूं, मुझे स्वीकार करो।

पीने का जल समर्पित करते समय निम्न मंत्र का उच्चारण करें-

ऊँ समस्तदेवदेवेशि सर्वतृप्तिकरं परम्।
अखंडानन्दसम्पूर्णं गृहाण जलमुत्तमम्॥

ऊँ ह्रीं श्रीं क्रीं परमेश्वरि कालिके नमः पानार्थं जलमं समर्पयामि।

अर्थात्-जो समस्त देवों में सर्वोपरि है, एवं अखंड परमानन्द की संपूर्णता की कारक है, उस देवी के पीने हेतु हम यह जल अर्पित करते हैं। इस जल सहित हे समृद्धि। वृद्धि व विघटन की देवि महाकालिका! मैं स्वयं को भी तुम्हें समर्पित करता हूं, कृपया मुझे स्वीकार करें।

ताम्बूल पत्र अर्थात् पान का पत्ता चढ़ाते समय निम्न मंत्र का उच्चारण करें-

पूंगीफलं महद्दिव्यं नागवल्ली दलैर्युतम्।
एलादिचूर्णसंयुक्तं ताम्बूलं प्रतिगृह्यताम्॥

ऊँ ह्रीं श्रीं क्रीं परमेश्वरि कालिके नमः ताम्बूलं समर्पयामि।

अर्थात्-यह पान का पत्ता, जो महान व शगुन स्वरूप है, जो कि नाग की तरह

Baandhava Shiva Bhaktaashcha Swadesho Bhuvanatrayam!!

Aum Hreem Shreem Kreem Parameshwari Kaalike Namah Bhoga Naivedya Samarpayaami!!

(Meaning) O Goddess! May the variety of choicest food items that are served in this extremely clean utensil give you best of satisfaction. O Goddess of Food, Annapoorna, you are perfect in all respects; you are the messenger of peace and the life breath of Mahashiva. O Goddess! Grant us knowledge, profit, sense of forgiveness, discretion and perfection. We bow reverentially to you. Our Mother is Devi Parvati and Father Lord Maheshwar. We the devotees of Lord Shiv and the master of all that is good and noble, invoke the Lord. I surrender myself unto you with all these oblations. O Goddess of all growth, decay and prosperity, kindly accept these along with me.

While offering the water for drinking to the Goddess chant the following mantra:

Aum Samastdevadevesh Sarva Triptikaram Param!

Akhanda Nanda Sampoorna Grihaan Jala Muttamam!!

Aum Hreem Shreem Kreem Parmeshwari Kaalike Namah

Panaarth Jalam Samarpayaami!

(Meaning) We offer this water for the drinking of that Goddess who is best among all the deities, and the very cause of granting us the universal bliss in perfectness. With this, O Goddess of all growth, decay and prosperity, I also offer myself to your shelter. Please accept me and all these libations.

While offering the betel leaf, chant the following mantra:

Pungiphalam Mahaddityam Naagvalli Daleiryutam!

Elaadi Churna Samyuktam Tamboolam Prati Grihaytaam!!

Aum Hreem Shreem Kreem Parmeshwari

Kaalike Namah Tamboolam Samarpayaami!!

(Meaning) This betel leaf, which is greatly auspicious and grown on the snake-like creeper for your honour, is offered to you for cleansing your mouth, Goddess. I offer it for this very purpose to you. Please accept it. I offer myself also to your shelter along with this betel leaf to you, O Goddess of

प्रतीत होने वाली लता पर से लाया गया है, हे देवि! तुम्हारे मुख की शुद्धता व निर्मलता हेतु तुम्हें अर्पित करता हूं, कृपया इसे ग्रहण करो। इस ताम्बूल पत्र के सहित हे समृद्धि! वृद्धि व विघटन की महादेवि! कालिका मैं स्वयं को भी तुम्हें समर्पित करता हूं, मुझे स्वीकार करो।

दक्षिणा अर्पित करते समय निम्न मंत्र का उच्चारण करें-

ऊँ पूजाफलसमृद्ध्यर्थं तवाग्रे स्वर्णमीश्वरि।
स्थापितं तेन ये प्रीता पूर्णान् कुरु मनोरथान्॥
हिरण्यगर्भगर्भस्थं हेमबीजं विभावसोः।
अनन्तपुण्यफलदमतः शान्तिं प्रयच्छ मे॥

ऊँ ह्रीं श्रीं क्रीं परमेश्वरि कालिके नमः दक्षिणां समर्पयामि।

अर्थात्-इस पूजन के फल को बढ़ाने हेतु हे धन की देवि मैं तुम्हें मेरी सर्वप्रिय वस्तु समर्पित करता हूं। मेरे मनोरथ की पूर्ति करना। हे परम् गर्भ की देवि! तुम्हारे गर्भ में समस्त प्राणियों के गर्भ अवस्थित हैं, जो तुम्हारे चमकते बीजों से उत्पन्न हुए हैं। जिस अखंड शांति का पाठ हम कर रहे हैं उसमें पूर्ण योग्यता प्रदान कर हमारा मनोरथ सफल करो। हे समृद्धि, वृद्धि व विघटन की महादेवि कालिका इस दक्षिणा सहित मैं स्वयं को भी तुम्हें समर्पित करता हूं, हमें स्वीकार करो।

□□□

all growth, decay and prosperity. Please accept all the offerings.

Now, while offering the Dakshina (the fees of the ritual) Chant the following mantra:

Aum Poojaphalasamriddhayartha Tavaagre Swarna Meeshwari!

Sthaapitam Ten ye Preeta Poornaan Kuru Manopathaan!

Hiranyagarbha Gar Bhastham Hemabeejam Vibhaavasoh!

Ananta Punya Phaladamatah Shantim Prayochcha Me!

Aum Hreem Shreem Kreem Parameshwari Kalike Namah Dakshinam Samarpayaami!!

(Meaning): O Goddess, I offer you my dearest thing that I have to you, for ensuring the enhanced benefit from this worship. O Goddess, all the beings and this whole universe repose in your womb only, which came into being through your shining seeds. Please grant us entire success in this ritual worship that we offer to you and fulfil our all desires. O Great Goddess Kalika, the goddess of all growth, decay and prosperity, I also offer you myself with this fees—please accept all the offerings.

❑❑❑

श्रीमहाकाली कवच

शिव उवाच

अर्थात्-श्री महेश्वर महाशिव जी ने कहा-

कथितं परमं ब्रह्मप्रकृतेः स्तवनं महत्।
आद्यायाः श्रीकालिकायाः कवचं शृणु साम्प्रतम्॥1॥

अर्थात्-परम ब्रह्माजी ने जो सत्य वचन परम आदरणीय अंधेरों को मिटाने वाली महाकालिका देवी के लिए कहे थे। मैं उस काली का कवच कहता हूं।

त्रैलोक्यविजयस्यास्य कवचस्य ऋषिः शिवः।
छन्दोऽनुष्टुब्देवता च आद्या काली प्रकीर्तिता॥2॥

अर्थात्-इस कवच को कहने वाले त्रिलोक विजेता महाशिव हैं। इसके छंद अनुष्टुप् है व इसकी देवी अंधेरों को दूर करने वाला महाकाली हैं।

मायाबीजं बीजमिति रमा शक्तिरुदाहृता।
क्रीं कीलकं काम्यसिद्धौ विनियोगः प्रकीर्तितः॥3॥

अर्थात्-माया का मूल मंत्र ही प्रमुख है। सुंदरता ही प्रसन्नता की ऊर्जा है।

हीमाद्या मे शिरः पातु श्री काली वदनं मम।
हृदयं क्रीं परा शक्तिः पायात् कण्ठं परात्परा॥4॥

अर्थात्-हे देवि! तुम ही प्रमुख हो, तुम मेरे मस्तक की रक्षा करो। जो देवि अंधकारों को दूर करती है वह कालीदेवि मेरे मुख की रक्षा करें। हे विघटन की देवी तुम मेरे हृदय में शक्ति बनकर विराजमान हो जाओ। एवं समस्त देवों की देवी मेरे कंठ में विद्यमान हो कर मेरी वाणी की रक्षा करो।

नेत्रे पातु जगद्धात्री कर्णौ रक्षतु शंकरी।
घ्राणं पातु महामाया रसनां सर्वमंगला॥5॥

अर्थात्-इस सृष्टि व इन्द्रियों को रचने वाली हे देवि मेरे नेत्रों में विद्यमान होकर मेरी नेत्र ज्योति की रक्षा करो। एवं शांति की देवी शंकरी तुम मेरे कानों की रक्षा करो। चेतना को सीमित करने वाली देवी महामाया मेरी नासिका की रक्षा करें। हे कल्याणमयी मेरी जिह्वा (स्वाद) की रक्षा करो।

Shree Mahakali Kavach

Shree Sadashiv Uvaach:

(Lord Eternal Shiv said):

Kathitam Paramam Brahma Prakateih Stuvanam Mahat।
Aadyaayaah Shree Kaalikayah Kavacham Shrunu Saampratאam।।1।।

Now I say that Kali Kavach, the one which Lord Brahma had uttered for invoking Maha Kali for eliminating the darkness.

Trailokya Vijayasyaasya Kavachasya Rishi Shivah।
Chhandoanustupdevata cha Aadya Kali Prakeertitah।।2।।

Lord Shiva the victor of all the three realms, Mahashiva is the narrator of this Kali Kavach. Its metre (of rhyme) is Anushtup and its deity is Mahakali, the eliminator of all the darkness.

Mayabeejam Beejamiti Rama Shakti Rudahrita।
Kreem Keelakam Kamyasiddhau Viniyogah Prakeertitah।।3।।

Maya's basic incantation is supreme and beauteousness' energy is happiness.

Heemaadyaa Me Shirah Paatu Shreem Kali Vadanam Mam।
Hridayam Kreem Parashakti Paayaat Kantham Paratpara।।4।।

O Goddess, you are supreme. You must protect my head. The Goddess Devi who eliminates darkness should protect my face. O Goddess of decay, you please repose in my heart as the source of all strength. And O Goddess of all the gods, you must repose yourself in my throat to protect ever my voice.

दन्तान रक्षतु कौमारी कपोलौ कमलालया।
ओष्ठाधरौ क्षमा रक्षेत् चिबुकं चारुहासिनी॥6॥

अर्थात्-हे शुद्धता की देवी कौमारी तुम मेरे दांतों की रक्षा करो। हे कमलामयी! तुम मेरे कपोलों (गालों) की रक्षा करो। क्षमामयी तुम मेरे होठों की व हे चारुहासिनी तुम मेरी ठोड़ी की रक्षा करो।

ग्रीवां पायात् कुलेशानी ककुत् पातु कृपामयी।
द्वौ बाहू बाहुदा रक्षेत् करौ कैवल्यदायिनी॥7॥

अर्थात्-हे परम महामयी! मेरी ग्रीवा (गर्दन) की रक्षा करो। एवं जो परमोपकार की अभिव्यक्ति है वह मेरी ऊपर वाली पीठ की रक्षा करे। बल प्रदान करने वाली देवी मेरी दोनों भुजाओं की रक्षा करें व हे कैवल्यदायिनी! तुम मेरे दोनों हाथों की रक्षा करो।

स्कन्धौ कपर्दिनी पातु पृष्ठं त्रैलोक्यतारिणी।
पार्श्वे पायादपर्णा मे कटिं मे कर्मठासना॥8॥

अर्थात्-वह जो अत्यंत भयानक है वह मेरे दोनों कंधों की रक्षा करे। वह जो त्रिलोकों को प्रदीप्त करती हैं, वह मेरी पीठ की रक्षा करे। वह जो अविभाज्य है, मेरी सभी तरफ से सुरक्षा करे। वह जो शक्ति व सामर्थ्य में विद्यमान है, वह मेरी कमर की रक्षा करे।

नाभौ पातु विशालाक्षी प्रजास्थानं प्रभावती।
ऊरुं रक्षतु कल्याणी पादौ मे पातु पार्वती॥9॥

अर्थात्-विशाल नेत्रों वाली देवी मेरी नाभि की रक्षा करे। जो प्रत्यक्ष प्रकाश की देवी है, वह प्रभावती मेरे लैंगिक अंग प्रदेश की रक्षा करे। जो कल्याणमयी है वह मेरी जंघाओं की एवं स्वयं पार्वती देवी मेरे दोनों चरणों की सुरक्षा करें।

जयदुर्गाऽवतु प्राणान् सर्वाङ्ग सर्वसिद्धिदा।
रक्षाहीनं तु यत् स्थानं वर्जितं कवचेन च॥10॥

अर्थात्-जय दुर्गे! देवी तुम मेरे श्वास व प्राण-ऊर्जा व समस्त सिद्धियों की सुरक्षा करो। वह देवी जो समस्त उपलब्धियां प्रदान करती है, वह मेरे पूरे शरीर व सभी अंगों की सुरक्षा करे। इस कवच के निपठन के दौरान जो स्थान वर्जित है अथवा जिनका उल्लेख नहीं किया है देवी उनकी भी रक्षा करें।

तत् सर्वं मे सदा रक्षेदाद्या काली सनातनी।
इति ते कथितं दिव्यं त्रैलोक्यविजयाभिधम्॥11॥

अर्थात्-मैं सदैव ही उस देवी की सुरक्षा में रहूं जो प्रमुख व चिरस्थायी एवं ईश्वररूप में विद्यमान हैं। वह जो समस्त अंधेरों को दूर करती है। यह उस दिव्य

Netre Paatu Jagatdhaatri Karnau Rakshatu Shankaree **|**

Pranam Paatu Mahamaya Rasana Sarva Mangala **||5||**

O Goddess, the curator of the world and shrubs, please repose in my eyes to protect my eyes' vision. And O Goddess of peace, Devi Shankaree, you must protect my ears. The Goddess Mahamaya, the ultimate limit of consciousness, may protect my nose. O welfare endower, protect my tongue (taste buds)!

Dantaan Rakshatu Kaumaari Kapolau Kamalaalaya **|**

Oshthadharau Kshama Rakshet Chibukam, Charuhaasini **||6||**

O Goddess of all piety, Kaumaari Devi, please protect my teeth. O Kamalaamayi, you must protect my cheeks. O Kshamamayi, you should protect my lips and O Charuhasini, protect my chin.

Greevan Paayaat Kuleshaani Kakut Paatu Kripaamayi **|**

Dwo Bahu Bahuda Rakshet Karau Kaivalyadaayini **||7||**

O Param Mahamayi! Protect my neck and she who is the manifestation of all the noble sentiments of altruism, protect my upper back. May the Goddess, the granter of all strength, protect my both arms and O Kaivalyadaayini, protect my both the hands.

Skandau Kapirdini Paatu Prishtham Trailokya Taarini **|**

Paarsvei Payaadar Prana Me Kati Me Kamathaasana **||8||**

She who is terribly frightening may protect my both the shoulders. She who keeps all the realms lighted may protect my back. She who is indivisible from any side may ensure my protection from every side and she who exists in all the power and capability may protect my waist.

Nabhau Paatu Vishaalaakshi Prajasthpnam Prabhavati **|**

Urum Rakshatu Kalyani Padaume Paatu Paarvati **||9||**

May the Goddess with large eyes protect my navel region. May the Goddess of light, Prabhavati, protect my

देवी के ज्ञान का स्पष्टीकरण है, जिनको तीनों लोकों पर विजय प्राप्त है।

कवचं कालिकादेव्यां आद्यायाः परमाद्भुतम्॥12॥

अर्थात्-यह उस देवी का कवच है जो चिरस्थायी ईश्वरीय माता है एवं जो समस्त अंधेरों को दूर करने वाली काली माता है।

पूजाकाले पठेद्यस्तु आद्याधिकृतमानसः।
सर्वान् कामानवाप्नोति तस्याद्या सुप्रसीदति॥
मन्त्रसिद्धिर्भवेदाशु किङ्कराः क्षुद्रसिद्धयः॥13॥

अर्थात्-जो जातक प्रातःकाल पूजा के समय नित्य अति भक्ति भावना से देवी का आवाहन अथवा इस कवच का पाठ करता है, उसकी समस्त मनोकामनाओं की पूर्ति होती है। संपूर्ण अर्पण से पूर्ण उपलब्धि की पूर्णता होती है व तुच्छ आहुति न दान एवं समर्पण से लघु उपलब्धि की प्राप्ति होती है।

अपुत्रो लभते पुत्रं धनार्थी प्राप्नुयाद्धनम्।
विद्यार्थी लभते विद्यां कामी कामनवाप्नुयात्॥14॥

अर्थात्-इस कवच का पाठ करने से जिनके घर में संतान नहीं होती वह संततिवान बन जाते हैं। जिनके पास धन की हानि होती है, उनकी इच्छाओं की भी पूर्ति होती है। विद्यार्थियों को विद्या का दान व इच्छुक जातकों के समस्त मनोरथ पूर्ण हो जाते हैं।

सहस्रावृत्तपाठेन वर्मणोऽस्य पुरस्क्रिया।
पुरश्चरणसंपन्न यथोक्तफलदं भवेत्॥15॥

अर्थात्-इस कवच का सहस्त्र बार पाठ करना एक बार हवन करने के समान फलदायक है।

चन्दनागरुकस्तूरीकुङ्कुमैः रक्तचन्दनैः।
भूर्जे विलिख्य गुटिकां स्वर्णस्थां धारयेद् यदि॥16॥

अर्थात्-चन्दन की लकड़ी, कस्तूरी, कुमकुम व लाल चन्दन चूर्ण को मिलाकर जातक को इस मंत्र को एक बार पेड़ की छाल अथवा सोने की प्लेट पर लिख कर धारण करना चाहिए। इससे उसे अत्यंत लाभ पहुंचता है।

शिखायां दक्षिणे बाहौ कण्ठे वा साधकः कटौ।
तस्याऽऽद्या कालिका वश्या वाञ्छितार्थं प्रयच्छति॥17॥

अर्थात्-सिर की शिखा पर, दाहिने हाथ, कंठ व कमर की कालिका देवी, जो सभी अंधेरों को मिटाती है, रक्षा करें व जातक को मनोवांछित फल प्रदान करें।

न कुत्रापि भयं तस्य सर्वत्र विजयी कविः।
अरोगी चिरंजीवी स्यात् बलवान् धारणक्षमः॥18॥

privities region. May Kalyanamayi protect my thigh region and Goddess Parvati herself my both the feet.

***Jayadurgaavatu Praandan Sarvaang Sarva Sidhada* I**

***Raksha Heenanto Yat Sthaanam Varjitam Kavachena Cha* I I*10* I I**

Victory to thee Dugra Devi! Please protect my life breath and all the Siddhis that I posses. That Goddess who provides all the achievement may protect my body and all organs. May she also protect my those parts which have not been referred to in this prayer or which are not mentionable.

***Tat Sarva Me Sada Rakshedadya Koli Sanatani* I**

***Iti Te Kathitam Divyam Trailokya Vijay Bhidham* I I*11* I I**

May I always stay under the protection of that Devi who is eternal and supreme and existent like Mother Goddess of the world; that who removes all the darkness. This whole universe is the exposition of Her manifestation who is the victor of all the three realms.

***Kavacham Kalika Devyam Aadyayah Param-adbhuvam* I I*12* I I**

This is the Kavach of that Devi Kali who removes all darkness and who is Eternal Divine Mother.

***Poojakale Pathedyastu Aadyadhi Krita Manasah* I**

***Sarvan Kamanvaapnoto Tasyadya Supraseedati* I I**

***Mantra Siddha Bhave Daashu Kinkarah Khvdra Siddhayah* I I*13* I I**

The aspirant who chants (or studies or recites) this Kavach with full feeling every morning after respectfully invoking the Goddess has all desires fulfilled. With total surrender unto the Goddess he gets total reward and with limited offerings or surrender he receives limited rewards.

***Aputro Labhate Putram Dhanarthi Praponuyadha Namah* I**

***Vidyaarthee Labhate Vidyam Kaami Kaman Vapnuyaat* I I*14* I I**

Those who read (or chant) this Kavach have their desires fulfilled; the issueless get children, the moneyless get riches; the students get good education. Thus they who read this Kavacha get their ambitions realized.

अर्थात्–इस कवच का पाठ करने से जातक के सभी प्रकार के भय दूर होकर विजय की प्राप्ति होती है, रोगी निरोगी होकर चिरंजीवी हो जाते हैं। कमज़ोर व्यक्ति बलवान हो जाता है।

सर्वविद्यासु निपुणः सर्वशास्त्रार्थतत्त्ववित्।
वशे तस्य महीपाला भोगमोक्षौ करस्थितौ॥19॥

अर्थात्–ऐसा जातक अति विद्वान व सभी शास्त्रों में निपुण हो जाता है। उसकी बुद्धि कुशाग्र हो जाती है। ऐसे जातक को संपूर्ण ब्रह्मांड से सुरक्षा व अंत में मोक्ष की प्राप्ति होती है। अतएव वह संपूर्ण जीवन सुखी सम्पन्न व्यतीत करता है।

कलिकल्मषयुक्तानां निःश्रेयसकरं परम्॥20॥

अर्थात्–अब इस परम ज्ञान को जानने के लिए आप सक्षम हैं जो गहरे अंधेरों को नष्ट करने में भी समर्थ है।

❑❑❑

Sahastra Vritta Pathena Varmanoasya Puraskriya I
Purashcharan Sampanna Yathokta Phaladam Bhavet I I 15 I I

Reading a thousand times this Kavach is equivalent to doing the havan once [i.e. the reward is the same].

Chandanaagaru Kasturi Kunkumei Raktachandaneih I
Bhoorje Vilakhya Gutikam Swarnasthan Dharyed Yadi I I 16 I I

This Kavach if written on the bark of the Bhoj Tree with the help of a sandalwood piece, vermilion and red sandalwood powder (mixed to a pasts form) or on the plate of gold would give much reward to the person who does it.

Shikhaayan Dakshine Bahau Kanthe Va Sadhakah Katau I
Tasyaaddyaa Kaalika Vashya Vaanchitaarth Prayachhi Ti I I 17 I I

Kalika Devi removes darkness from everywhere ruling from the crown of the head, from the right hand and the waist and she may protect the aspirant and grant him (or her) with the desired results.

Na Kutrapi Bhayam Tasya Sarvatra Vijayi Kavih I
Arogi Chirajeevi Syat Balwaan Dharanaksham I I 18 I I

The reading of this Kavach removes all the fears of the aspirant and grants him victory in every mission. Such persons remain diseaseless and long-aged; even those who are weak become strong.

Sarva Vidyasu Nipunah Sarva Shaastrarth Tatva Vid I
Vashe Tasya Maheepala Bhoga Mokhau Karasthitau I I 19 I I

Such a native (the one who reads it) becomes a very erudite scholar well versed in all scriptural disciplines. He develops a very sharp and powerful brain. He receives protection in the entire world and at last also receives salvation (Moksha). This way he passes his entire life in prosperity and happiness.

Kali Kalmash Yuktaanam Nihshreyaskaram Param I I 20 I I

Now you are capable of knowing this Supreme Knowledge which destroys all the filth of this Kali Age and removes all darkness of ignorance. ❑❑❑

श्रीमहाकाली अष्टोत्तरसहस्त्र नामावली

श्मशानकालिका काली भद्रकाली कपालिनी।
गुह्यकाली महाकाली कुरुकुल्लाविरोधिनी।।1।।

(1) श्मशान कालिका (2) काली
(3) भद्रकाली (4) कपालिनी
(5) गुह्यकाली (6) महाकाली
(7) कुरुकुल्लाविरोधिनी

कालिका कालरात्रिश्च महाकाल नितम्बिनी।
काल भैरव भार्या च कुलवर्त्मप्रकाशिनी।।2।।

(8) कालिका (9) कालरात्रि
(10) महाकालनितम्बिनी (11) कालभैरव भार्या
(12) कुलवर्त्मप्रकाशिनी

कामदा कामिनी काम्या कमनीयस्वभाविनी।
कस्तूरीरसलिप्तांगी कुञ्जरेश्वरगामिनी।।3।।

(13) कामदा (14) कामिनी
(15) काम्या (16) कमनीय स्वभाविनी
(17) कस्तूरीरसलिप्तांगी (18) कुञ्जरेश्वरगामिनी

ककारवर्णसर्वांगी कामिनी कामसुन्दरी।
कामार्ता कामरूपा च कामधेनुः कलावती।।4।।

(19) ककारवर्णसर्वांगी (20) कामिनी
(21) कामसुन्दरी (22) कामार्ता
(23) कामरूपा (24) कामधेनु
(25) कलावती

कान्ता कामस्वरूपा च कामाख्या कुलपालिनी।
कुलीना कुलवत्यम्बा दुर्गा दुर्गार्तिनाशिनी।।5।।

(26) कान्ता (27) कामस्वरूपा
(28) कामाख्या (29) कुलपालिनी

Thousand and Eight Names of Goddess Mahakali

Smashaan Kalika Kali Bhadrakali Kapalini I
Guhyakali Mahakali Kurukullaavirodhini I I 1 I I

1. Shmashaan Kaalika
2. Kali
3. Bhadrakali
4. Kapaalini
5. Guhyakali
6. Mahakali
7. Kurukullaavirodhini

Kaalika Kaalaraatrishya Mahakaal Nitambini
Kaal Bhairav Bharya Cha Kulavatmr Prakaashini I I 2 I I

8. Kaalika
9. Kaalraatri
10. Mahakaalanijambini
11. Kaal Bhairav Bharya
12. Kulavatmr Prakashini

Kaamda Kaamini Kaamya Kamaneeya Swabhaavini
Kasturirasa Liptaangi Kunjreshwara Gaamini I I 3 I I

13. Kaamda
14. Kaamini
15. Kaamya
16. Kamaneeya Swabhaavini
17. Kasturirasa Liptaangi
18. Kunjreshwara Gaamini

Kakaar Varnasarvaangi Kamini Kamsundari
Kaamarta Kaamroopa Cha Kaamdhenuh Kalavati I I 4 I I

19. Kakaar Varnasarvaangi
20. Kaamini
21. Kaamsundari
22. Kaamarta
23. Kamroopa
24. Kaamdhenu
25. Kalavati

Kanta Kaamswaroopa Cha Kamakhya Kulapaalini I
Kuleena Kulavatyamba Durga Durgati Naashini I I 5 I I

26. Kanta
27. Kaamswaroopa
28. Kamaakhya
29. Kulapaalini
30. Kuleena
31. Kulavatyamba
32. Durga
33. Durgati Naashini

(30) कुलीना (31) कुलवत्यम्बा

(32) दुर्गा (33) दुर्गार्तिनाशिनी

कुमारी कुलजा कृष्णा कृष्णदेहा कृशोदरा।
कृशांगी कुलिशांगी च क्रींकारी कमला कला॥6॥

(34) कुमारी (35) कुलजा

(36) कृष्णा (37) कृष्णदेहा

(38) कृशोदरा (39) कृशांगी

(40) कुलिशांगी (41) क्रींकारी

(42) कमला (43) कला

करालास्या कराली च कुलकान्ताऽपराजिता।
उग्रा उग्रप्रभा दीप्ता विप्रचित्ता महानना॥7॥

(44) करालास्या (45) कराली

(46) कुलकान्ताऽपराजिता (47) उग्रा

(48) उग्रप्रभा (49) दीप्ता

(50) विप्रचित्ता (51) महानना

नीलाधना वलाका च मात्रा मुद्रामितासिता।
ब्राह्मी नारायणी भद्रा सुभद्रा भक्तवत्सला॥8॥

(52) नीलाधना (53) वलाका

(54) मात्रा (55) मुद्रामितासिता

(56) ब्राह्मी (57) नारायणी

(58) भद्रा (59) सुभद्रा

(60) भक्तवत्सला

माहेश्वरी च चामुण्डा वाराही नारसिंहिका।
वज्राङ्गी वज्रकङ्काली नृमुण्डस्रग्विणी शिवा॥19॥

(61) माहेश्वरी (62) चामुण्डा

(63) वाराही (64) नारसिंहिका

(65) वज्राङ्गी (66) वज्रकङ्काली

(67) नृमुण्डस्रग्विणी (68) शिवा

मालिनी नरमुण्डाली गलत्रुधिरभूषणा।
रक्तचन्दनसिक्ताङ्गी सिन्दूरारुणमस्तका॥10॥

(69) मालिनी (70) नरमुण्डाली

(71) गलत्रुधिरभूषणा (72) रक्तचन्दनस्रिक्ताङ्गी

Kumari Kulaja Krishna Krishnadeha Krishodara I
Krishaangi Kulishaangi Cha Kreenkari Kamala Kala I I6I I

34. Kumari
35. Kulaja
36. Krishna
37. Krishnadeha
38. Krishodara
39. Krishaangi
40. Kulishaangi
41. Kreenkari
42. Kamala
43. Kala

Karaalasya Karali Cha Kulakantaaparajita I
Ugra Ugraprabha Deepta Viprachitra Mahanana I I7I I

44. Karaalasya
45. Karali
46. Kulakantaaparajita
47. Ugra
48. Ugraprabha
49. Deepta
50. Viprachitra
51. Mahaanana

Neelaghana Valaka Cha Maatra Mudra Mitasita I
Brahmi Narayani Bhadra Subhadra Bhakta-vatsala I I8I I

52. Neelaghana
53. Valaka
54. Maatra
55. Mudra Mitasita
56. Brahmi
57. Narayani
58. Bhadra
59. Subhadra
60. Bhaktavatsala

Maheshwari Va Chamunda Varaahi Naarsinhika I
Vajraangi Vajrakankali Nrimundaa Srigivaani Shiva I I9I I

61. Maheshwari
62. Chamunda
63. Varaahi
64. Naarsinhikaa
65. Vajraangi
66. Vajrakankali
67. Nrimundraa Srigivaani
68. Shiva

Mālinī Naramuṇḍālī Galatrudhirabhūṣaṇa
Raktachandanasiktāngī Sindūrāruṇamastakā I I10I I

69. Mālinī
70. Naramuṇḍālī
71. Galatrudhirabhusana
72. Raktachandanasiktangi
73. Sindūrāruṇamastakā

Ghorarūpā Ghoradaṃstrā Ghorāghoratarā Śubhā
Mahādaṃṣṭrā Mahāmāya Sudantī Yugadanturā I I11I I

74. Ghoraṛūpā
75. Ghoradaṃṣṭrā
76. Ghorāghoratarā
77. Śubhā
78. Mahādaṃṣṭrā
79. Mahāmāyā
80. Sudantī
81. Yugadanturā

(73) सिन्दूरारुणमस्तका

घोररूपा घोरदंष्ट्रा घोराघोरतरा शुभा।
महादंष्ट्रा महामाया सुदन्ती युगदन्तुरा॥11॥

(74)घोररूपा (75)घोरदष्ट्रा
(76)घोराघोरतरा (77)शुभा
(78)महादंष्ट्रा (79)महामाया
(80)सुदन्ती (81)युगदन्तुरा

सुलोचना विरूपाक्षी विशालाक्षी त्रिलोचना।
शारदेन्दुप्रसन्नास्या स्फुरत्स्मेराम्बुजेक्षणा॥12॥

(82)सुलोचना (83)विरूपक्षी
(84)विशालाक्षी (85)त्रिलोचना
(86)शारदेन्दुप्रसन्नास्या (87)स्फुरत्स्मेराम्बुजेक्षणा

अट्टहासप्रसन्नास्या स्मेरवक्त्रा सुभाषिणी।
प्रसन्नपद्मवदना स्मितास्या प्रियभाषिणी॥13॥

(88)अट्टहासप्रसन्नास्या (89)स्मेरवक्त्रा
(90)सुभाषिणी (91)प्रसन्नपद्मवदना
(92)स्मितास्या (93)प्रियभाषिणी

कोटराक्षी कुलश्रेष्ठा महती बहुभाषिणी।
सुमतिः कुमतिश्चण्डा चण्डमुण्डातिवेगिनी॥14॥

(94) कोटराक्षी (95) कुलश्रेष्ठा
(96) महती (97) बहुभाषिणी
(98) सुमति (99) कुमति
(100) चंडा (101) चण्डमुण्डातिवेगिनी

प्रचण्डचण्डिका चण्डी चण्डिका चण्डवेगिनी।
सुकेशी मुक्तकेशी च दीर्घकेशी महत्कुचा॥15॥

(102) प्रचंडचंडिका (103) चंडी
(104) चंडिका (105) चंडवेगिनी
(106) सुकेशी (107) मुक्तकेशी च
(108) दीर्घकेशी (109) महत्कुचा

प्रेतदेहकर्णपूरा प्रेतपाणिसुमेखला।
प्रेतासना प्रियप्रेता प्रेतभूमिकृतालया॥16॥

(110) प्रेतदेहकर्णपूरा (111) प्रेतपाणिसुमेखला

Sulochana Viūpākṣī Visālākṣī Trilochanā
Śāradenduprasannasyā Sphuratsmerambujekṣaṇā | |12| |

82. Sulochanā
83. Virūpākṣī
84. Viśālākṣī
85. Trilochana
86. Śāradenduprasannāsyā
87. Sphuratsmerāmbujekṣaṇā

Aṭṭahāsaprasannāyā Smeravaktrā Subhāṣiṇī
Prasannapadmavadana Smitasya Priyabhasini | |13| |

88. Aṭṭahāsaprasannāsyā
89. Smeravaktrā
90. Subhāṣiṇī
91. Prasannapadmavadanā
92. Smitāsyā
93. Priyabhāṣiṇī

Koṭarākṣī Kulaśreṣṭhā Mahatī Bahubhāṣiṇi
Sumatih Kumatischaṇḍā Chaṇḍamuṇḍātiveginī | |14| |

94. Koṭarākṣī
95. Kulaśreṣṭā
96. Mahatī
97. Bahubhāṣiṇi
98. Sumatih
99. Kumatih
100. Chaṇḍā
101. Chaṇḍamuṇḍātiveginī

Prachaṇḍacandikā Chandī Chandika Chandaveginī
Sukesi Muktakeśī Cha Dirghakeśī Mahatkuchā | |15| |

102. Pracaṇḍacaṇḍikā
103. Chaṇḍī
104. Chaṇḍikā
105. Chaṇḍaveginī
106. Sukeśī
107. Muktakesi
108. Dīrghakeśī
109. Mahatkuchā

Pretadehakarnapūrā Pretāpaṇisumekhalā
Pretāsanā Priyapretā Pretabhūmikṛtālayā | |16| |

110. Pretadehakarṇapūrā
111. Pretapāṇisumekhalā
112. Pretāsanā
113. Priyapretā
114. Pretabhūmikṛtālayā

Śmaśānāvasinī Puṇyā Puṇyadā Kulapaṇḍitā
Puṇyālayā Puṇyadehā Punyaślokā Cha Pāvinī | |17| |

115. Śmaśanavāsinī
116. Punyā
117. Puṇyadā
118. Kulapaṇḍitā
119. Puṇyālayā
120. Puṇyadehā
121. Puṇyaślokā
122. Pāvinī

Pūtā Pavitrā Parāma Purāpunyavibhūsaṇā
Puṇyanāmnī Bhitiharā Varadā Khangapalini | |18| |

123. Pūtā
124. Pavitrā
125. Paramā
126. Purāpunyavibhūṣaṇā
127. Punyanāmni
128. Bhītiharā

(112) प्रेतासना (113) प्रियप्रेता
(114) प्रेतभूमिकृतालया

श्मशानवासिनी पुण्या पुण्यदा कुलपण्डिता।
पुण्यालया पुण्यदेहा पुण्यश्लोका च पाविनी॥17॥

(115) श्मशानवासिनी (116) पुण्या
(117) पुण्यदा (118) कुलपंडिता
(119) पुण्यालया (120) पुण्यदेहा
(121) पुण्यश्लोका (122) पाविनी

पूता पवित्रा परमा पुरापुण्यविभूषणा।
पुण्यनाम्नी भीतिहरा वरदा खड्गपालिनी॥18॥

(123) पूता (124) पवित्रा
(125) परमा (126) पुरापुण्यविभूषणा
(127) पुण्यनाम्नी (128) भीतिहरा
(129) वरदा (130) खड्गपालिनी

नृमुण्डहस्तशस्ता च छिन्नमस्ता सुनासिका।
दक्षिणा श्यामला श्यामा शान्ता पीनोन्नतस्तनी॥19॥

(131) नृमुण्डहस्तशस्ता (132) छिन्नमस्ता
(133) सुनासिका (134) दक्षिणा
(135) श्यामला (136) श्यामा
(137) शान्ता (138) पीनोन्नतस्तनी

दिगम्बरा घोररावा सृक्कान्ता रक्तवाहिनी।
घोररावा शिवासंगी विसंगी मदनातुरा॥20॥

(139) दिगम्बरा (140) घोररावा
(141) सृक्कान्ता (142) रक्तवाहिनी
(143) घोररावा (144) शिवासंगी
(145) विसंगी (146) मदनातुरा

मत्ता प्रमत्ता प्रमदा सुधासिन्धुनिवासिनी।
अतिमत्ता महामत्ता सर्वाकर्षणकारिणी॥21॥

(147) मत्ता (148) प्रमत्ता
(149) प्रमदा (150) सुधासिन्धुनिवासिनी
(151) अतिमत्ता (152) महामत्ता
(153) सर्वाकर्षणकारिणी

129. Varadā 130. Khangapalini

Nrmuṇḍahastaśastā Cha Chinnamastā Sunāsikā
Dakṣiṇā Syāmalā Syāmā Sāntā
Pīnonnatastanī I I 19 I I

131. Nṛmuṇḍahastasastā 132. Chinnamastā
133. Sunāsikā 134. Daksiṇā
135. Śyāmalā 136. Śyāmā
137. Śāntā 138. Pīnonnatastanī

Digambarā Ghorarāvā Srkkāntā Raktavāhinī
Ghorarāvā Sivāsaṃgi Visaṃgi Madanāturā I I 20 I I

139. Digambarā 140. Ghorarāvā
141. Srkkāntā 142. Raktavāhinī
143. Ghorarāvā 144. Śivāsaṃgī
145. Visamgi 146. Madanatura

Mattā Pramattā Pramada Sudhāsindhunivāsinī
Atimattā Mahāmattā Sarvākarṣṇakāriṇi I I 21 I I

147. Mattā 148. Pramattā
149. Pramadā 150. Sudhāsindhunivāsinī
151. Atimattā 152. Mahāmattā
153. Sarvākarṣaṇakārinī

Gītapriyā Vādyaratā Pretanṛtyaparāyaṇā
Chaturbhujā Daśabhujā Aṣṭādaśabhujā Tathā I I 22 I I

154. Gītapriyā 155. Vādyaratā
156. Pretanṛtyaparāyaṇā 157. Chaturbhujā
158. Daśabhujā
159. Aṣṭadaśabhujā tathā

Kātyāyanī Jaganmātā Jagatāṃ Parameśvarī
Jagadbandhurjagaddhātrī
Jagadānandākariṇī I I 23 I I

160. Kātyāyanī 161. Jaganmātā
162. Jagatāṃ Parameśvari
163. Jagadbandhuḥ 164. Jagaddhātrī
165. Jagadānandakāriṇī

Jagajjīvamayī Haimavatī Māyā Mahāmahī
Nāgayajñopavītāngī Nāgini Nāgaśāyinī I I 24 I I

166. Jagajjīvamayī 167. Haimavatī
168. Māyā 169. Mahāmahī
170. Nāgayajñopavītāngī
171. Nāginī 172. Nāgaśāyinī

गीतप्रिया वाद्यरता प्रेतनृत्यपरायणा।
चतुर्भुजा दशभुजा अष्टादशभुजा तथा॥22॥

(154) गीतप्रिया (155) वाद्यरता
(156) प्रेतनृत्यपरायणा (157) चतुर्भुजा
(158) दशभुजा (159) अष्टादशभुजा तथा

कात्यायनी जगन्माता जगतां परमेश्वरी।
जगद्बन्धुर्जगद्धात्री जगदानन्दकारिणी॥23॥

(160) कात्यायनी (161) जगन्माता
(162) जगता परमेश्वरी (163) जगद्बन्धुः
(164) जगद्धात्री (165) जगदानन्दकारिणी

जगज्जीवमयी हैमवती माया महामही।
नागयज्ञोपवीताङ्गी नागिनी नागशायिनी॥24॥

(166) जगज्जीवमयी (167) हैमवती
(168) माया (169) महामही
(170) नागयज्ञोपवीताङ्गी (171) नागिनी
(172) नागशायिनी

नागकन्या देवकन्या गन्धर्वी किन्नरेश्वरी।
मोहरात्रिर्महारात्रिर्दारुणा भास्वरासुरी॥25॥

(173) नागकन्या (174) देवकन्या
(175) गन्धर्वी (176) किन्नरेश्वरी
(177) मोहरात्रि (178) महारात्रि
(179) दारुणा (180) भास्वरासुरी

विद्याधरी वसुमती यक्षिणी योगिनी जरा।
राक्षसी डाकिनी वेदमयी वेदविभूषणा॥26॥

(181) विद्याधरी (182) वसुमती
(183) यक्षिणी (184) योगिनी
(185) जरा (186) राक्षसी
(187) डाकिनी (188) वेदमयी
(189) वेदविभूषणा

Nāgakanyā Devakanyā Gandharvī Kinnareśvarī
Moharātrirmahārātrirdāruṇā Bhāsvarāsurī||25||

173. Nāgakanyā
174. Devakanyā
175. Gandharvī
176. Kinnareśvarī
177. Moharātrih
178. Mahārātrih
179. Dāruṇā
180. Bhāsvarāsurī

Vidyādharī Vasumatī Yaksiṇī Yoginī Jarā
Rākṣaśī Dākinī Vedamayī Vedavibhūṣaṇā||26||

181. Vidyādharī
182. Vasumatī
183. Yakṣiṇi
184. Yoginī
185. Jarā
186. Rākṣasī
187. Dākinī
188. Vedamayī
189. Vedavibhūṣaṇā

Śrutiḥ Smṛtirmahāvidyā Guhyavidyā Purātanī
Chintyā-Chintyā Svadhā Svāhā Nidrā Tandrā Cha
Pārvatī||27||

190. Sritiḥ
191. Smṛtiḥ
192. Mahāvidyā
193. Guhyavidyā
194. Purātanī
195. Chintyā
196. Achhintyā
197. Svadhā
198. Svāhā
199. Nidrā
200. Tandrā
201. Pārvatī

Aparṇā Niśchalā Lolā Sarvavidyā Tapasvinī
Gaṃga Kaśi Śachi Sitā Satī Satyaparāyaṇā||28||

202. Aparṇā
203. Niśchalā
204. Lolā
205. Sarvavidyā
206. Tapasvinī
207. Gaṃgā
208. Kāśī
209. Śachī
210. Sītā
211. Satī
212. Satyaparāyaṇā

Nītiḥ Sunītiḥ Suruchistuṣṭiḥ Puṣṭirdhṛtiḥ Kṣamā
Vāṇī Buddhirmahālakṣmīrlakṣmirnlasarasvatī||29||

213. Nītiḥ
214. Sunītiḥ
215. Suruchiḥ
216. Tuṣṭiḥ
217. Puṣṭiḥ
218. Dhṛtiḥ
219. Kṣamā
220. Vāṇī
221. Buddhiḥ
222. Mahālakṣmīḥ
223. Lakṣmīḥ
224. Nīlasarasvatī

Srotasvatī Sarasvatī Mātaṃgī Vijayā Jayā
Nadī Sindhuḥ Sarvamayī Tārā Śūnyanivāsinī||30||

225. Srotasvatī
226. Sarasvatī
227, Mātaṃgī
228. Vijayā

श्रुतिः स्मृतिर्महाविद्या गुह्यविद्या पुरातनी।
चिन्त्याऽचिन्त्या स्वधा स्वाहा निद्रा तन्द्रा च पार्वती।।27।।

(190) श्रुति
(191) स्मृति
(192) महाविद्या
(193) गुह्यविद्या
(194) पुरातनी
(195) चिन्त्या
(196) अचिन्त्या
(197) स्वधा
(198) स्वाहा
(199) निद्रा
(200) तन्द्रा
(201) पार्वती

अपर्णा निश्चला लोला सर्वविद्या तपस्विनी।
गंगा काशी शची सीता सती सत्यपरायणा।।28।।

(202) अपर्णा
(203) निश्चला
(204) लोला
(205) सर्वविद्या
(206) तपस्विनी
(207) गंगा
(208) काशी
(209) शची
(210) सीता
(211) सती
(212) सत्यपरायणा

नीतिः सुनीतिः सुरुचिस्तुष्टिः पुष्टिर्धृतिः क्षमा।
वाणी बुद्धिर्महालक्ष्मीर्लक्ष्मीर्नीलसरस्वती।।29।।

(213) नीति
(214) सुनीति
(215) सुरुचि
(216) तुष्टि
(217) पुष्टि
(218) धृति
(219) क्षमा
(220) वाणी
(221) बुद्धि
(222) महालक्ष्मी
(223) लक्ष्मी
(224) नीलसरस्वती

स्रोतस्वती सरस्वती मातंगी विजया जया।
नदी सिन्धुः सर्वमयी तारा शून्यनिवासिनी।।30।।

(225) स्रोतस्वती
(226) सरस्वती
(227) मातंगी
(228) विजया
(229) जया
(230) नदी सिन्धु
(231) सर्वमयी
(232) तारा
(233) शून्यनिवासिनी

229. Jayā
230. Nadī Sindhuḥ
231. Sarvamayī
232. Tārā
233. Śūnyanivāsinī

Śuddhā Taranginī Medhā Lākinī Bahurūpinī
Sthūlā Sūkṣmā Sūkṣmatarā
Bhagavatyanurāgiṇī I I 31 I I

234. Śuddhā
235. Tarangiṇī
236. Medhā
237. Lākinī
238. Bahurūpiṇī
239. Sthūlā
240. Sūkṣmā
241. Sūkṣmatarā
242. Bhagvatī
243. Anurāgiṇī

Paramānandarūpā Cha Chidānandasvarūpiṇī
Sarvānandamayī Nityā Sarvānandasvarūpiṇī I I 32 I I

244. Paramānandarūpā
245. Chidānandasvarūpiṇī
246. Sarvānanmdamayī
247. Nityā
248. Sarvānandasvarūpiṇī

Śubhadā Nandinī Stutyā Stavanīyasvasvabhāvinī
Raṃkiṇi Bhaṃkini Chitrā Vichitra
Chitrarūpiṇi I I 33 I I

249. Śubhdā
250. Nandinī
251. Stutyā
252. Stavanīyasvabhāvinī
253. Raṃkiṇī
254. Bhaṃkinī
255. Chitrā
256. Vichitrā
257. Chitrarūpiṇī

Padmā Padmālayā Pdmamukhī Padmavibhūsaṇa
Hākinī Sākinī Śāntā Rākiṇī Rudhirapriyā I I 34 I I

258. Padmā
259. Padmālayā
260. Padmamukhī
261. Padmavibhūṣaṇā
262. Hākinī
263. Śākinī
264. Śantā
265. Rākiṇī
266. Rudhirapriyā

Bhrāntirbhavānī Rudrāṇī Mṛdānī Śatrumardinī
Upendrāṇī Mahendrāṇī Jyotsnā
Chandrasvarūpiṇī I 35 I I

267. Bhrāntiḥ
268. Bhavānī
269. Rudrāṇī
270. Mṛḍānī
271. Śatrumardinī
272. Upendrānī
273. Mahendrānī
274. Jyotsna
275. Chandrasvrūpiṇī

शुद्धा तरङ्गिणी मेधा लाकिनी बहुरूपिणी।
स्थूला सूक्ष्मा सूक्ष्मतरा भगवत्यनुरागिणी॥31॥

(234) शुद्धा (235) तरङ्गिणी
(236) मेधा (237) लाकिनी
(238) बहुरूपिणी (239) स्थूला
(240) सूक्ष्मा (241) सूक्ष्मतरा
(242) भगवती (243) अनुरागिणी

परमानन्दरूपा च चिदानन्दस्वरूपिणी।
सर्वानन्दमयी नित्या सर्वानन्दस्वरूपिणी॥32॥

(244) परमानन्दरूपा (245) चिदानन्दस्वरूपिणी
(246) सर्वानन्दमयी (247) नित्या
(248) सर्वानन्दस्वरूपिणी

शुभदा नन्दिनी स्तुत्या स्तवनीचस्वभाविनी।
रंकिणी भंकिनी चित्रा विचित्रा चित्ररूपिणी॥33॥

(249) शुभदा (250) नन्दिनी
(251) स्तुत्या (252) स्तवनीयस्वभाविनी
(253) रंकिणी (254) भंकिनी
(255) चित्रा (256) विचित्रा
(257) चित्ररूपिणी

पद्मा पद्मालया पद्ममुखी पद्मविभूषणा।
हाकिनी शाकिनी शान्ता राकिणी रुधिरप्रिया॥34॥

(258) पद्मा (259) पद्मालया
(260) पद्ममुखी (261) पद्मविभूषणा
(262) हाकिनी (263) शाकिनी
(264) शान्ता (265) राकिणी
(266) रुधिरप्रिया

भ्रान्तिर्भवानी रुद्राणी मृडानी शत्रुमर्दिनी।
उपेन्द्राणी महेन्द्राणी ज्योत्स्ना चन्द्रस्वरूपिणी॥35॥

(267) भ्रान्ति (268) भवानी
(269) रुद्राणी (270) मृडानी
(271) शत्रुमर्दिनी (272) उपेन्द्राणी
(273) महेन्द्राणी (274) ज्योत्स्ना

Sūryātmikā Rudrapatnī Raudrī Strī Prakṛtiḥ Pumān Śaktiḥ Sūktirmatirmātā Bhuktirmuktiḥ Pativratā I I36 I I

276. Sūryātmikā
277. Rudrapatnī
278. Raudrī
279. Strī prakṛtiḥ
280. Pumān
281. Śaktiḥ
282. Sūktiḥ
283. Matiḥ
284. Mātā
285. Bhuktiḥ
286. Muktiḥ
287. Pativratā

Sarveśvarī Sarvamātā Śarvānī Haravallabhā Sarvajñā Siddhidā Siddhā Bhavyā Bhavyā Bhāyapahā I I37 I I

288. Sarveśvarī
289. Sarvamātā
290. Śarvāṇī
291. Haravallabhā
292. Sarvajñā
293. Siddhidā
294. Siddhā
295. Bhavyā
296. Bhāvyā
297. Bhayāphā

Kartrī Hartrī Pālayitrī Sarvarī Tāmasī Dayā Tamisrā Tāmasī Sthāṇuḥ Sthirā Dhīrā Tapasvinī I I38 I I

298. Kartrī
299. Hartrī
300. Pālayitrī
301. Sarvari
302. Tāmasī
303. Dayā
304. Tamisrā
305. Tāmasī
306. Sthāṇuḥ
307. Sthirā
308. Dhīrā
309. Tapasvinī

Chārvangī Chañcalā Lolajihvā Chāruchritriṇī Trapā Trapāvatī Lajjā Vilajjā Hriḥ Rajovatī I I39 I I

310. Chārvangī
311. Chañcalā
312. Lolajihvā
313. Chārucaritriṇī
314. Trapā
315. Trapāvatī
316. Lajjā
317. Vilajjā
318. Hrīḥ
319. Rajovatī

Sarasvatī Dharmaniṣṭhā Śresthā Niṣṭhuranādinī Gariṣṭhā Duṣṭasamhartrī Viśiṣṭa Śreyasī Ghṛṇa I I40 I I

320. Sarasvatī
321. Dharmaniṣṭhā
322. Śreṣṭhā
323. Niṣṭhuranādini
324. Gariṣṭha
325. Duṣṭasamhartrī

(275) चन्द्रस्वरूपिणी

सूर्यात्मिका रुद्रपत्नी रौद्री स्त्री प्रकृतिः पुमान्।
शक्तिः सूक्तिर्मतिर्माता भुक्तिर्मुक्तिः पतिव्रता॥36॥

(276) सूर्यात्मिका (277) रुद्रपत्नी
(278) रौद्री (279) स्त्री प्रकृति
(280) पुमान् (281) शक्ति
(282) सूक्ति (283) मति
(284) माता (285) भुक्ति
(286) मुक्ति (287) पतिव्रता

सर्वेश्वरी सर्वमाता शर्वाणी हरवल्लभा।
सर्वज्ञा सिद्धिदा सिद्धा भव्या भाव्या भयापहा॥37॥

(288) सर्वेश्वरी (289) सर्वमाता
(290) शर्वाणी (291) हरवल्लभा
(292) सर्वज्ञा (293) सिद्धिदा
(294) सिद्धा (295) भव्या
(296) भाव्या (297) भयापहा

कर्त्री हर्त्री पालयित्री शर्वरी तामसी दया।
तमिस्रा तामसी स्थाणुः स्थिरा धीरा तपस्विनी॥38॥

(298) कर्त्री (299) हर्त्री
(300) पालयित्री (301) शर्वरी
(302) तामसी (303) दया
(304) तमिस्रा (305) तामसी
(306) स्थाणु (307) स्थिरा
(308) धीरा (309) तपस्विनी

चार्वङ्गी चञ्चला लोलजिह्वा चारुचरित्रिणी।
त्रपा त्रपावती लज्जा विलज्जा ह्रीः रजोवती॥39॥

(310) चार्वङ्गी (311) चञ्चला
(312) लोलजिह्वा (313) चारुचरित्रिणी
(314) त्रपा (315) त्रपावती
(316) लज्जा (317) विलज्जा
(318) ह्री (319) रजोवती

326. Visiṣṭa
327. Śreyasī
328. Ghṛṇā

Bhīmā Bhayānakā Bhīmnādinī Bhiḥ Prabhāvatī Vāgīśvarī Srīryamunā Yajñakartri Yajuhpriya I I41 I I

329. Bhīmā
330. Bhayānakā
331. Bhīmanādinī
332. Bhīh
333. Prabhāvatī
334. Vāgīsvarī
335. Śriḥ
336. Yamunā
337. Yajñakartrī
338. Yajuḥpriyā

Ṛksāmatharvanilayā Rāgiṇī Sobhanasvarā Kalakaṇṭhī Kambukaṇṭhī Veṇuviṇāparāyaṇā I I42 I I

339. Ṛksāmārthāvanilayā
340. Rāgiṇī
341. Śobhanasvarā
342. Kalakṇṭhī
343. Kambukaṇṭhī
344. Veṇuvīnāparāyaṇā

Vaṃśinī Vaiṣṇavī Svacchā Dharitrī Jagadisvarī Madhumatī Kuṇḍalini Ṛddhiḥ Śiddhiḥ Śuchismitā I I43 I I

345. Vaṃśinī
346. Vaiṣṇivī
347. Svacchā
348. Dharitrī
349. Jagadīśvarī
350. Madhumatī
351. Kuṇḍalinī
352. Ṛddhiḥ
353. Siddhiḥ
354. Śuchismitā

Rambhorvaśīratīramā Rohinī Revati Maghā Śaṅkhinī Chakriṇi Kṛṣṇā Gadinī Padminī Tathā I I44 I I

355. Rambhorvaśī
356. Ratī ramā
357. Rohiṇī
358. Revati
359. Maghā
360. Śaṅkhinī
361. Chakriṇi
362. Kṛṣṇā
363. Gadinī
364. Padminī tathā

Śūlinī Parighāstrā Cha Pāśinī Śārngapaninī Pinākadhāriṇī Dhūmrā Śarabhī Vanamālinī I I45 I I

365. Śūlinī
366. Parighastrā
367. Pāśinī
368. Śarṅgapāṇinī
369. Pinākadhāriṇī
370. Dhūmrā

सरस्वती धर्मनिष्ठा श्रेष्ठा निष्ठुरनादिनी।
गरिष्ठा दुष्टसंहर्त्री विशिष्टा श्रेयसी घृणा॥40॥

(320) सरस्वती (321) धर्मनिष्ठा
(322) श्रेष्ठा (323) निष्ठुरनादिनी
(324) गरिष्ठा (325) दुष्टसंहर्त्री
(326) विशिष्टा (327) श्रेयसी
(328) घृणा

भीमा भयानका भीमनादिनी भीः प्रभावती।
वागीश्वरी श्रीर्यमुना यज्ञकर्त्री यजुःप्रिया॥41॥

(329) भीमा (330) भयानका
(331) भीमनादिनी (332) भी
(333) प्रभावती (334) वागीश्वरी
(335) श्री (336) यमुना
(337) यज्ञकर्त्री (338) यजुःप्रिया

ऋक्सामाथर्वनिलया रागिणी शोभनस्वरा।
कलकण्ठी कम्बुकण्ठी वेणुवीणापरायणा॥42॥

(339) ऋक्सामाथर्वनिलया (340) रागिणी
(341) शोभनस्वरा (342) कलकण्ठी
(343) कम्बुकण्ठी (344) वेणुवीणापरायणा

वंशिनी वैष्णवी स्वच्छा धरित्री जगदीश्वरी।
मधुमती कुण्डलिनी ऋद्धिः सिद्धिः शुचिस्मिता॥43॥

(345) वंशिनी (346) वैष्णवी
(347) स्वच्छा (348) धरित्री
(349) जगदीश्वरी (350) मधुमती
(351) कुंडलिनी (352) ऋद्धि
(353) सिद्धि (354) शुचिस्मिता

रम्भोर्वशीरतीरमा रोहिणी रेवती मघा।
शङ्खिनी चक्रिणी कृष्णा गदिनी पद्मिनी तथा॥44॥

(355) रम्भोर्वशी (356) रती रमा
(357) रोहिणी (358) रेवती
(359) मघा (360) शङ्खिनी
(361) चक्रिणी (362) कृष्णा

371. Śarabhī
372. Vanamālinī

Rathinī Samaraprītā Veginī Raṇapaṇḍitā
Jaṭinī Vajriṇī Līlā Lāvaṇyāmbudhichandrikā||46||

373. Rethinī
374. Samaraprītā
375. Veginī
376. Ranapaṇḍita
377. Jatini
378. Vajrini
379. Līlā
380. Lāvaṇyāmbudhichandrikā

Balipriyā Sadāpūjyā Pūrṇā Daityendramathinī
Mahiṣāsurasaṃhartrī Kāminī raktadantikā||47||

381. Balipriyā
382. Sadāpūjyā
383. Pūrṇā
384. Daityendramathinī
385. Mahiṣāsurasaṃhartrī
386. Kāminī
387. Raktadantikā

Raktapā Rudhirāktāngī Raktakharparahastinī
Raktapriyā Māmsaruchirāsavāsaktamānasa||48||

388. Raktapā
389. Rudhiraktangī
390. Raktakharparahastinī
391. Raktapriyā
392. Māṁsaruchirāsavāsaktamānasā

Galacchonitamuṇḍālī Kaṇṭhamālavibhūṣaṇā
Śavāsanā Chitāntaḥsthā Māhesī Vṛṣavāhinī||49||

393. Galacchoṇitamṇḍālī
394. Kaṇṭhamālavibhūṣaṇā
395. Śavāsanā
396. Chitāntaḥsthā
397. Māheśī
398. Vṛṣavāhinī

Vyāghratvagambarā Chīnachailini Siṃhavāhinī
Vāmadevī Mahādevī Gaurī Sarvajñabhāminī||50||

399. Vyāghratvagmbarā
400. Chīnachailinī
401. Siṃhāvahinī
402. Vāmadevī

(363) गदिनी (364) पद्मिनी तथा

शूलिनी परिघास्त्रा च पाशिनी शार्ङ्गपाणिनी।
पिनाकधारिणी धूम्रा शरभी वनमालिनी।।45।।

(365) शूलिनी (366) परिघास्त्रा
(367) पाशिनी (368) शार्ङ्गपाणिनी
(369) पिनाकधारिणी (370) धूम्रा
(371) शरभी (372) वनमालिनी

रथिनी समरप्रीता वेगिनी रणपण्डिता।
जटिनी वज्रिणी लीला लावण्याम्बुधिचन्द्रिका।।46।।

(373) रथिनी (374) समरप्रीता
(375) वेगिनी (376) रणपंडिता
(377) जटिनी (378) वज्रिणी
(379) लीला (380) लावण्याम्बुधिचन्द्रिका

बलिप्रिया सदापूज्या पूर्णा दैत्येन्द्रमथिनी।
महिषासुरसंहर्त्री कामिनी रक्तदन्तिका।।47।।

(381) बलिप्रिया (382) सदापूज्या
(383) पूर्णा (384) दैत्येन्द्रमथिनी
(385) महिषासुरसंहर्त्री (386) कामिनी
(387) रक्तदन्तिका

रक्तपा रुधिराक्ताङ्गी रक्तखर्परहस्तिनी।
रक्तप्रिया मांसरुचिरासवासक्तमानसा।।48।।

(388) रक्तपा (389) रुधिराक्ताङ्गी
(390) रक्तखर्परहस्तिनी (391) रक्तप्रिया
(392) मांसरुचिरासवासक्तमानसा

गलच्छोणितमुण्डाली कण्ठमालाविभूषणा।
शवासना चितान्तःस्था माहेशी वृषवाहिनी।।49।।

(393) गलच्छोणितमुंडाली (394) कंठमालाविभूषणा
(395) शवासना (396) चितान्तःस्था
(397) माहेशी (398) वृषवाहिनी

व्याघ्रत्वगम्बरा चीनचैलिनी सिंहवाहिनी।
वामदेवी महादेवी गौरी सर्वज्ञभामिनी।।50।।

(399) व्याघ्रत्वगम्बरा (400) चीनचैलिनी

403. Mahādevī
404. Gaurī
405. Sarvajñabhāminī

Bālikā Taruṇī Vrddhā Vṛddhamātā Jarāturā Subhrūrvilāsinī Brahma Vādinī Brāhmaṇī Mahī||51||

406. Bālikā
407. Taruṇī
408. Vṛddhā
409. Vṛddhamātā
410. Jarāturā
411. Subhrūḥ
412. Vilāsinī
413. Brahmavādinī
414. Brāhmaṇī
415. Mahī

Svapnavatī Chitralekhā Lopāmudrā Suresvarī Amoghāruṇdhatī Tikṣṇā Bhogavatyanurāgiṇī||52||

416. Svapnavatī
417. Chitralekhā
418. Lopāmudrā
419. Sureśvarī
420. Amoghā
421. Arundhatī
422. Tīkṣṇā
423. Bhogavatī
424. Anurāginī

Mandākinī Mandahāsā Jvālāmukhyasurāntakā Mānadā Mānini Mānya Mānanīyā Madāturā||53||

425. Mandākini
426. Mandahāsā
427. Jvālāmukhī
428. Asurāntakā
429. Mānadā
430. Māninī
431. Mānyā
432. Mānaniyā
433. Madāturā

Madirā Meduronmādā Medhyā Sādhyā Prasādinī Sumabhyānantaguṇinī Sarvalokottamottamā||54||

434. Madirā Meduronmada

(401) सिंहवाहिनी
(402) वामदेवी
(403) महादेवी
(404) गौरी
(405) सर्वज्ञभामिनी

बालिका तरुणी वृद्धा वृद्धमाता जरातुरा।
सुभ्रूर्विलासिनी ब्रह्मवादिनी ब्राह्मणी मही॥51॥

(406) बालिका
(407) तरुणी
(408) वृद्धा
(409) वृद्धमाता
(410) जरातुरा
(411) सुभ्रू
(412) विलासिनी
(413) ब्रह्मवादिनी
(414) ब्राह्मणी
(415) मही

स्वप्नवती चित्रलेखा लोपामुद्रा सुरेश्वरी।
अमोघारुन्धती तीक्ष्णा भोगवत्यनुरागिणी॥52॥

(416) स्वप्नवती
(417) चित्रलेखा
(418) लोपामुद्रा
(419) सुरेश्वरी
(420) अमोघा
(421) अरुंधती
(422) तीक्ष्णा
(423) भोगवती
(424) अनुरागिणी

मन्दाकिनी मन्दहासा ज्वालामुख्यसुरान्तका।
मानदा मानिनी मान्या माननीया मदातुरा॥53॥

(425) मन्दाकिनी
(426) मन्दहासा
(427) ज्वालामुखी
(428) असुरान्तका
(429) मानदा
(430) मानिनी
(431) मान्या
(432) माननीया
(433) मदातुरा

मदिरा मेदुरोन्मादा मेध्या साध्या प्रसादिनी।
सुमध्यानन्तगुणिनी सर्वलोकोत्तमोत्तमा॥54॥

(434) मदिरा मेदुरोन्मादा
(435) मेध्या
(436) साध्या
(437) प्रसादिनी
(438) सुमध्यानन्तगुणिनी
(439) सर्वलोकोत्तमोत्तमा

जयदा जित्वरा जेत्री जयश्रीर्जयशालिनी।
शुभदा सुखदा सत्या सभासंक्षोभकारिणी॥55॥

(440) जयदा
(441) जित्वरा

435. Medhyā
436. Sādhyā
437. Prasādinī
438. Sumadhyanantaguṇinī
439. Sarvalokottamottamā

Jayadā Jitvarā Jetrī Jayaśrirjayaśalinī
Śubhadā Sukhadā Satyā
Sabhāsaṃksobhakāriṇī I I55I I

440. Jayadā
441. Jitvarā
442. Jutrī
443. Jayaśrīh
444. Jayaśālinī
445. Śubhadā
446. Sukhadā
447. Satyā
448. Sabhāsaṃkṣobhakārinī

Sivadūtī Bhūtimatī Vidhūtirbhīsaṇānanā
Kaumārī Kulajā Kuntī Kulastrī Kulapālikā I I56I I

449. Śivadūtī
450. Bhūtimatī
451. Vibhūtiḥ
452. Bhīsaṇānanā
453. Kaumārī
454. Kulajā
455. Kuntī
456. Kulastri
457. Kulapālikā

Kīrttir Yaśasvinī Bhūsā Bhūṣṭhā Bhūtapatipriyā
Saguṇā Nirguṇā Tṛṣṇā Niṣṭhā Kāṣṭhā
Pratiṣṭhita I I57I I

458. Kīrttiḥ
459. Yaśasvinī
460. Bhūṣā
461. Bhūṣṭhā
462. Bhūtapatipriyā
463. Saguṇā
464, Nirguṇā
465. Tṛṣṇā
466. Niṣṭhā
467. Kāṣṭhā
468. Pratiṣṭhita

Dhaniṣṭhā Dhanadā Dhānyā Vasudhā Suprakāśinī
Urvī Gurvī Gurusreṣṭhā Sadguṇā Triguṇātmikā I I58I I

469. Dhaniṣṭhā
470. Dhanadā
471. Dhānyā
472. Vasudhā
473. Suprakāśinī
474. Urvī
475. Gurvī
476. Guruśreṣṭhā
477. Sadguṇa
478. Triguṇātmikā

Rājñamājñā Mahāprajñā Saguṇa Nirgunātmikā
Mahākulīnā Niṣkāmā Sakāmā Kāmajīvanī I I59I I

479. Rājñamājñā
480. Mahāprajñā
481. Saguṇā
482. Nirguṇātmikā
483. Mahākulīnā
484. Niṣkāmā
485. Sakāmā
486. Kāmajīvanī

(442) जेत्री
(443) जयश्री
(444) जयशालिनी
(445) शुभदा
(446) सुखदा
(447) सत्या
(448) सभासंक्षोभकारिणी

शिवदूती भूतिमती विभूतिर्भीषगानना।
कौमारी कुलजा कुन्ती कुलस्त्री कुलपालिका॥56॥

(449) शिवदूती
(450) भूतिमती
(451) विभूति
(452) भीषणानना
(453) कौमारी
(454) कुलजा
(455) कुंती
(456) कुलस्त्री
(457) कुलपालिका

कीर्तिर्यशस्विनी भूषा भूष्ठा भूतपतिप्रिया।
सगुणा निर्गुणा तृष्णा निष्ठा काष्ठा प्रतिष्ठिता॥57॥

(458) कीर्ति
(459) यशस्विनी
(460) भूषा
(461) भूष्ठा
(462) भूतपतिप्रिया
(463) सगुणा
(464) निर्गुणा
(465) तृष्णा
(466) निष्ठा
(467) काष्ठा
(468) प्रतिष्ठिता

धनिष्ठा धनदा धान्या वसुधा सुप्रकाशिनी।
उर्वी गुर्वी गुरुश्रेष्ठा सद्‌गुणा त्रिगुणात्मिका॥58॥

(469) धनिष्ठा
(470) धनदा
(471) धान्या
(472) वसुधा
(473) सुप्रकाशिनी
(474) उर्वी
(475) गुर्वी
(476) गुरुश्रेष्ठा
(477) सद्‌गुणा
(478) त्रिगुणात्मिका

राज्ञामाज्ञा महाप्रज्ञा सगुणा निर्गुणामिका।
महाकुलीना निष्कामा सकामा कामजीवनी॥59॥

(479) राज्ञामाज्ञा
(480) महाप्रज्ञा
(481) सगुणा
(482) निर्गुणात्मिका
(483) महाकुलीना
(484) निष्कामा
(485) सकामा
(486) कामजीवनी

Kāmadevakalā Rāmābhirāmā Śivanartkī
Chintāmaṇiḥ Kalpalatā Jāgratī Dinavatsalā||60||

487. Kāmadevakalā
488. Rāmābhirāmā
489. Śivanartakī
490. Chintāmaṇiḥ
491. Kalpalatā
492. Jāgratī
493. Dīnavatsalā

Kārttkī Kṛtikā Kṛtyā Ayodhyā Viṣamāsamā
Sumantra Mantriṇī Pūrṇā Hlādinī Kleśanāśinī||61||

494. Kārttkī
495. Kṛtikā
496. Kṛtyā
497. Ayodhyā Viṣamāsamā
498. Sumantrā
499. Mantriṇī
500. Pūrṇā
501. Hlādini
502. Kleśanāsinī

Trailokyajananī Jyeṣṭhā Mīmāṃsāmantrarūpiṇī
Tadaganimnajathara Suskamamsasthimalini||62||

503. Trailokyajananī
504. Jyeṣṭhā
505. Mīmāṃsāmantrarūpiṇī
506. Taḍāganimnajaṭharā
507. Śuṣkamāṁsāsthimālinī

Avantīmathurāhṛdayā Trailokyapāvanakṣamā
Vyaktāvyaktātmikā Mūriṭh Sarabhī
Bhīmanādinī||63||

508. Avantīmathurāhrdayā
509. Trailokyapāvanakṣamā
510. Vyaktāvyaktātmikā mūrtih
511. Śarabhī bhīmanādinī

Ksemaṅkarī Śaṅkari Cha Sarvasammohakāriṇī
Ūrdhvatejasvini Klinnā Mahātejasvinī Tathā||64||

512. Kṣemaṅkarī
513. Sankarī
514. Sarvasammohakāriṇī
515. Ūrdhvatejasvinī
516. Klinnā
517. Mahātejasvinī Tatha

Advaitabhoginī Pūjyā Yuvatī Sarvamangalā
Sarvapriyaṅkari Bhogyā Dharaṇī Piśitaśanā||65||

518. Advaitabhoginī
519. Pūjyā
520. Yuvatī
521. Sarvamaṅgalā

कामदेवलका रामाभिरामा शिवनर्तकी।
चिन्तामणि: कल्पलता जाग्रती दीनवत्सला॥60॥

(487) कामदेवकला (488) रामाभिरामा
(489) शिवनर्तकी (490) चिंतामणि
(491) कल्पलता (492) जाग्रती
(493) दीनवत्सला

कार्तिकी कृतिका कृत्या अयोध्या विषमासमा।
सुमन्त्रा मन्त्रिणी पूर्णा ह्लादिनी कलेशनाशिनी॥61॥

(494) कार्तिकी (495) कृतिका
(496) कृत्या (497) अयोध्या विषमासमा
(498) सुमन्त्रा (499) मंत्रिणी
(500) पूर्णा (501) ह्लादिनी
(502) क्लेशनाशिनी

त्रैलोक्यजननी ज्येष्ठा मीमांसामन्त्ररूपिणी।
तडागनिम्नजठरा शुष्कमांसास्थिमालिनी॥62॥

(503) त्रैलोक्यजननी (504) ज्येष्ठा
(505) मीमांसामन्त्ररूपिणी (506) तडागनिम्नजठरा
(507) शुष्कमांसास्थिमालिनी

अवन्तीमथुराहृदया त्रैलोक्यपावनक्षमा।
व्यक्ताव्यक्तात्मिका मूर्ति: शरभी भीमनादिनी॥63॥

(508) अवन्तीमथुराहृदया (509) त्रैलोक्यपावनक्षमा
(510) व्यक्ताव्यक्तात्मिका मूर्ति (511) शरभी भीमनादिनी

क्षेमङ्करी शङ्करी च सर्वसम्मोहकारिणी।
ऊर्ध्वतेजस्विनी क्लिन्ना महातेजस्विनी तथा॥64॥

(512) क्षेमङ्करी (513) शङ्करी
(514) सर्वसम्मोहकारिणी (515) ऊर्ध्वतेजस्विनी
(516) क्लिन्ना (517) महातेजस्विनी

अद्वैतभोगिनी पूज्या युवती सर्वमङ्गला।
सर्वप्रियङ्करी भोग्या धरणी पिशिताशना॥65॥

(518) अद्वैतभोगिनी (519) पूज्या
(520) युवती (521) सर्वमङ्गला
(522) सर्वप्रियङ्करी (523) भोग्या

522. Sarvapriyaṅkari
523. Bhogyā
524. Dharanī
525. Piśitāśanā

Bhayamkarī Pāpaharā Niṣkalamkā Vaśaṃkarī
Āśā Tṛṣṇā Chandrakalā Indrānī Vāyuveginī| |66| |

526. Bhayaṃkarī
527. Pāpaharā
528. Niṣkalaṃkā
529. Vaśaṃkarī
530. Āśā
531. Tṛṣṇā
532. Chandrakalā
533. Indrānī
534. Vāyuveginī

Sahasrasūrysamkāśā Chandrakotisamaprabhā
Niśumbhaśumbhasaṃhantrī
Raktabījavināśinī| |67| |

535. Sahasrasūryasaṃkāśā
536. Chandrakotisamaprabhā
537. Niśumbhaśumbhasaṃhantrī
538. Raktabījavināśinī

Madhukaiṭabhahantrī Cha Mahiṣāsuraghātinī
Vahnimaṇḍalamadhyasthā Sarvasattvapratiṣṭhitā| |68| |

539. Madhukaiṭabhahantrī
540. Mahiṣāsuraghātinī
541. Vahnimaṇḍalamadhyasthā
542. Sarvasattvapratiṣṭhitā

Sarvāchāravatī Sarvadevakanyādhidevatā
Dakṣakanyā Dakṣayajñanāśinī Durgatāriṇī| |69| |

543. Sarvāchāravatī
544. Sarvadevakanyādhidevatā
545. Dakṣakanyā
546. Dakṣayajñanāśinī
547. Durgatāriṇī

Ijyā Pūjyā Vibhīrbhūtiḥ Satkīrttirbrahmarūpinī
Rambhorūśchaturākārā Jayantī Karuṇā Kuhūḥ| |70| |

548. Ijyā
549. Pūjyā
550. Vibhīrbhūtiḥ
551. Satkīrttiḥ
552. Brahmrūpiṇī
553. Rambhorūḥ
554. Chaturākāra
555. Jayantī
556. Karuṇā
557. Kuhūḥ

Manasvinī Devamātā Yaśasyā Brahmacārinī
Siddhaidā Vṛddhidā Vrddhiḥ Sarvādyā Sarvadāyinī| |71| |

558. Manasvinī
559. Devamātā
560. Yaśasya
561. Brahmachāriṇī

(524) धरणी (525) पिशिताशना

भयंकरी पापहरा निष्कलंका वशंकरी।

आशा तृष्णा चन्द्रकला इन्द्राणी वायुवेगिनी॥66॥

(526) भयंकरी (527) पापहरा

(528) निष्कलंका (529) वशंकरी

(530) आशा (531) तृष्णा

(532) चन्द्रकला (533) इन्द्राणी

(534) वायुवेगिनी

सहस्रसूर्यसंकाशा चन्द्रकोटिसमप्रभा।

निशुम्भशुम्भसंहन्त्री रक्तबीजविनाशिनी॥67॥

(535) सहस्रसूर्यसंकाशा (536) चन्द्रकोटिसमप्रभा

(537) निशुम्भशुम्भसंहंत्री (538) रक्तबीजविनाशिनी

मधुकैटभहन्त्री च महिषासुरघातिनी।

वह्निमण्डलमध्यस्था सर्वसत्त्वप्रतिष्ठिता॥68॥

(539) मधुकैटभहन्त्री (540) महिषासुरघातिनी

(541) वह्निमण्डलमध्यस्था (542) सर्वसत्त्वप्रतिष्ठिता

सर्वाचारवती सर्वदेवकन्याधिदेवता।

दक्षकन्या दक्षयज्ञनाशिनी दुर्गतारिणी॥69॥

(543) सर्वाचारवती (544) सर्वदेवकन्याधिदेवता

(545) दक्षकन्या (546) दक्षयज्ञनाशिनी

(547) दुर्गतारिणी

इज्या पूज्या विभीर्भूतिः सत्कीर्त्तिर्ब्रह्मरूपिणी।

रम्भोरूश्चतुराकारा जयन्ती करुणा कुहूः॥70॥

(548) इज्या (549) पूज्या

(550) विभीर्भूति (551) सत्कीर्ति

(552) ब्रह्मरूपिणी (553) रम्भोरू

(554) चतुराकारा (555) जयन्ती

(556) करुणा (557) कुहू

मनस्विनी देवमाता यशस्या ब्रह्मचारिणी।

सिद्धिदा वृद्धिदा बुद्धिः सर्वाद्या सर्वदायिनी॥71॥

(558) मनस्विनी (559) देवमाता

(560) यशस्या (561) ब्रह्मचारिणी

562. Siddhadā
563. Vṛddhidā
564. Vṛddhiḥ
565. Sarvādyā
566. Sarvadāyinī

Agādharūpiṇī Dhyeya Mūlādhāranivāsinī
Ājñā Prajñā Pūrṇamanaś Chandramukhyanukūlinī I I72 I I

567. Agādharūpiṇī
568. Dhyeyā
569. Mūlādhāranivāsinī
570. Ajñā
571. Prajñā
572. Pūrṇamanāḥ
573. Chandramukhyanukūlinī

Vāvadūkā Nimnanābhiḥ Satyasandhā Dṛḍhavratā
Anvīkṣikī Daṇḍanītistrayī Tridivasundarī I I73 I I

574. Vāvadūkā
575. Nimnanābhih
576. Satyasandhā
577. Dṛḍhavratā
578. Anvikṣikī
579. Daṇḍanīti
580. Trayī
581. Tridivasundarī

Jvalini Jvalinī Sailatanayā Vindhyavāsinī
Pratyayā Khecharī Dhairyā Turīyā Vimalāturā I I74 I I

582. Jvalinī
583. Jvālinī
584. Śailatanayā
585. Vindhyavāsinī
586. Pratyayā
587. Khecharī
588. Dhairyā
589. Turīyā
590. Vimalāturā

Pragalbhā Vāruṇīcchāyā Śaśinī Visphulinginī
Bhaktiḥ Siddhiḥ Sadā Prītiḥ Prākāmyā Mahimāṇimā I I75 I I

591. Pragalbhā
592. Vāruṇīcchāyā
593. Śaśinī
594. Visphulinginī
595. Bhaktiḥ
596. Siddhiḥ
597. Sadāprītiḥ
598. Prākāmyā
599. Mahimāṇimā

Icchāsiddhir Vasitvā Cha Iśitvordhvanivāsinī
Laghimā Chaiva Gāyatrī Sāvitrī Bhuvaneśvarī I I76 I I

600. Icchāsiddhiḥ
601. Vaśitvā
602. Īśitvordhvanivāsinī
603. Laghimā Chaiva
604. Gayatrī
605. Sāvitrī
606. Bhuvaneśvarī

Manoharā Chitā Divyā Devyudārā Manoramā
Pingalā Kapilā Jihvā Rasajñā Rasikā Ramā I I77 I I

607. Manoharā
608. Chitā
609. Divyā
610. Devyudārā
611. Manoramā
612. Pingalā
613. Kapilā
614. Jihvārasajñā
615. Rasikā
616. Ramā

(562) सिद्धिदा (563) वृद्धिदा
(564) वृद्धि (565) सर्वाद्या
(566) सर्वदायिनी

अगाधरूपिणी ध्येया मूलाधारनिवासिनी।
आज्ञा प्रज्ञा पूर्णमनाश्चन्द्रमुख्यनुकूलिनी॥72॥

(567) अगाधरूपिणी (568) ध्येया
(569) मूलाधारनिवासिनी (570) आज्ञा
(571) प्रज्ञा (572) पूर्णमना
(573) चन्द्रमुख्यनुकूलिनी

वावदूका निम्ननाभिः सत्यसन्धा दृढव्रता।
आन्वीक्षिकी दण्डनीतिस्त्रयी त्रिदिवसुन्दरी॥73॥

(574) वावदूका (575) निम्ननाभि
(576) सत्यसंधा (577) दृढव्रता
(578) आन्वीक्षिकी (579) दंडनीति
(580) त्रयी (581) त्रिदिवसुंदरी

ज्वलिनी ज्वालिनी शैलतनया विन्ध्यवासिनी।
प्रत्यया खेचरी धैर्या तुरीया विमलातुरा॥74॥

(582) ज्वलिनी (583) ज्वालिनी
(584) शैलतनया (585) विन्ध्यवासिनी
(586) प्रत्यया (587) खेचरी
(588) धैर्या (589) तुरीया
(590) विमलातुरा

प्रगल्भा वारुणीच्छाया शशिनी विस्फुलिङ्गिनी।
भक्तिः सिद्धिः सदा प्रीतिः प्राकाम्या महिमाणिमा॥75॥

(591) प्रगल्भा (592) वारुणीच्छाया
(593) शशिनी (594) विस्फुलिङ्गिनी
(595) भक्ति (596) सिद्धि
(597) सदाप्रीति (598) प्राकाम्या
(599) महिमाणिमा

इच्छासिद्धिर्वशित्वा च ईशित्वोर्ध्वनिवासिनी।
लघिमा चैव गायत्री सावित्री भुवनेश्वरी॥76॥

(600) इच्छासिद्धि (601) वशित्वा

Susumneḍāyogavatī Gāndhārī Narakāntakā Pañchalī Rumiṇi Rādhā Rādhyā Bhāmā cha Rādhikā I I78I I

617. Suṣumneḍāyogavatī
618. Gāndhārī
619. Narakāntakā
620. Pāñchālī
621. Rukmiṇi
622. Rādhā
623. Radhyā
624. Bhāmā
625. Rādhikā

Amṛtā Tulasī Vṛndā Kaiṭabhī Kapateśvarī Ugrachaṇḍeśvarī Vīrajananī Vīrasundarī I I79I I

626. Amṛtā
627. Tulasī
628. Vṛndā
629. Kaiṭabhī
630. Kapaṭesvarī
631. Ugrachaṇdesvarī
632. Vīrajananī
633. Vīrasundarī

Ugratārā Yaśodākhyā Devakī Devamānitā Niraṃjanā Chitā Devī Krodhinī Kuladipikā I I80I I

634. Ugratārā
635. Yaśodākhyā
636. Devakī
637. Devamānitā
638. Niraṃjanā chitā
639. Devī
640. Krodhinī
641. Kuladīpikā

Kulavāgiśvarī Jvālā Mātṛkā Drāvaṇī Dravā Yogeśvarī Mahāmārī Bhrāmarī Bindurūpiṇī I I81I I

642. Kulavāgīśvarī
643. Jvālā
644. Mātṛkā
645. Drāvaṇī
646. Dravā
647. Yogeśvarī
648. Mahāmārī
649. Bhrāmarī
650. Bindurūpiṇī

Dūtī Prāneśvarī Guptā Bahulā Ḍāmarī Prabhā Kubjikā Jñanini Jyestha Bhusundi Prakatakrtih I I82I I

651. Dūtī
652. Prāṇesvarī
653. Guptā
654. Bahulā
655. Dāmarī
656. Prabhā
657. Kubjikā
658. Jñāninī
659. Jyeṣṭha
660. Bhusuṇḍī

(602) ईशित्वोर्ध्वनिवासिनी (603) लघिमा
(604) गायत्री (605) सावित्री
(606) भुवनेश्वरी

मनोहरा चिता दिव्या देव्युदारा मनोरमा।
पिङ्गला कपिला जिह्वा रसज्ञा रसिका रमा॥77॥

(607) मनोहरा (608) चिता
(609) दिव्या (610) देव्युदारा
(611) मनोरमा (612) पिङ्गला
(613) कपिला (614) जिह्वारसज्ञा
(615) रसिका (616) रमा

सुषुम्नेडायोगवती गान्धारी नरकान्तका।
पाञ्चाली रुक्मिणी राधा राध्या भामा च राधिका॥78॥

(617) सुषुम्नेडायोगवती (618) गान्धारी
(619) नरकान्तका (620) पाञ्चाली
(621) रुक्मिणी (622) राधा
(623) राध्या (624) भामा
(625) राधिका

अमृता तुलसी वृन्दा कैटभी कपटेश्वरी।
उग्रचण्डेश्वरी वीरजननी वीरसुन्दरी॥79॥

(626) अमृता (627) तुलसी
(628) वृंदा (629) कटभी
(630) कपेटश्वरी (631) उग्रचंडेश्वरी
(632) वीरजननी (633) वीरसुन्दरी

उग्रतारा यशोदाख्या देवकी देवमानिता।
निरंजना चिता देवी क्रोधिनी कुलदीपिका॥80॥

(634) उग्रतारा (635) यशोदाख्या
(636) देवकी (637) देवमानिता
(638) निरंजना चिता (639) देवी
(640) क्रोधिनी (641) कुलदीपिका

कुलवागीश्वरी ज्वाला मातृका द्रावणी द्रवा।
योगेश्वरी महामारी भ्रामरी विन्दुरूपिणी॥81॥

(642) कुलवागीश्वरी (643) ज्वाला

661. Prakaṭākrtih

Drāviṇī Gopinī Māyā Kāmabījeśvarī Priyā
Śākambharī Kokanadā Suśilā Cha Tilottamā I I83 I I

662. Drāviṇi
663. Gopinī
664. Māyā
665. Kāmabījeśvarī
666. Priyā
667. Śākambharī
668. Kokanadā
669. Suśīlā
670. Tilottamā

Ameyavikramākrurā Sampacchīlātivikramā
Svastihavyavahā Prītirūsmā Dhūmrārchirangadā I I84 I I

671. Ameyavikramākrūrā
672. Sampacchīlātivikramā
673. Svastihavyavahā
674. Prīti
675. Ūṣmā
676. Dhūmrārchirangadā

Tapinī Tāapinī Viśvā Bhogadā Bhogadhārinī
Trikhaṇḍā Bodhinī Vaśyā Sakalā Viśvarūpiṇī I I85 I I

677. Tapinī
678. Taapinī
679. Visvā
680. Bhogadā
681. Bhogadhāriṇī
682. Trikhaṇḍā
683. Bodhinī
684. Vaśyā
685. Sakalā
686. Visvarūpiṇī

Bījarūpā Mahāmudrā Vaśinī Yogarūpinī
Anangakusumā Naṅgamekhalā-Nangarūpiṇī I I86 I I

687. Bījarūpā
688. Mahāmudrā
689. Vaśinī
690. Yogarūpiṇī
691. Anaṅgakusumā
692. Anaṅgamekhlā
693. Anaṅgarūpiṇī

Anangamadanā-Naṅgarekhā-Naṅgāṅkuśeśvarī
Anaṅgamālinī Kāmeśvarī Sarvārthasādhikā I I87 I I

694. Anaṅgamadanā
695. Anaṅgarekhā
696. Anaṅgāṅkuṣesvarī
697. Anaṅgamālinī
698. Kameśvarī
699. Sarvārthasādhikā

(644) मातृका (645) द्रावणी

(646) द्रवा (647) योगेश्वरी

(648) महामारी (649) भ्रामरी

(650) बिन्दुरूपिणी

दूती प्राणेश्वरी गुप्ता बहुला डामरी प्रभा।
कुब्जिका ज्ञानिनी ज्येष्ठा भुशुण्डी प्रकटाकृतिः॥82॥

(651) दूती (652) प्राणेश्वरी

(653) गुप्ता (654) बहुला

(655) डामरी (656) प्रभा

(657) कुब्जिका (658) ज्ञानिनी

(659) ज्येष्ठा (660) भुशुंडी

(661) प्रकटाकृति

द्राविणी गोपिनी माया कामबीजेश्वरी प्रिया।
शाकम्भरी कोकनदा सुशीला च तिलोत्तमा॥83॥

(662) द्राविणी (663) गोपिनी

(664) माया (665) कामबीजेश्वरी

(666) प्रिया (667) शाकंभरी

(668) कोकनदा (669) सुशीला

(670) तिलोत्तमा

अमेयविक्रमाक्रूरा सम्पच्छीलातिविक्रमा।
स्वस्तिहव्यवहा प्रीतिरूष्मा धूम्रार्चिरङ्गदा॥84॥

(671) अमेयविक्रमाक्रूरा (672) सम्पच्छीलातिविक्रमा

(673) स्वस्तिहव्यवहा (674) प्रीति

(675) ऊष्मा (676) धूम्रार्चिरङ्गदा

तपिनी तापिनी विश्वा भोगदा भोगधारिणी।
त्रिखण्डा बोधिनी वश्या सकला विश्वरूपिणी॥85॥

(677) तपिनी (678) तापिनी

(679) विश्वा (680) भोगदा

(681) भोगधारिणी (682) त्रिखंडा

(683) बोधिनी (684) वश्या

(685) सकला (686) विश्वरूपिणी

Sarvatamtramayī Modinyaruṇānāngarūpiṇī
Vajreśvarī Cha Javanī
Sarvaduḥkhākṣayaṃkarī | |88| |

700. Sarvataṃtramayī
701. Modinyaruṇanaṅgarūpiṇī
702. Vajreśvarī
703. Jananī
704. Sarvaduḥkhakṣayaṃkarī

Sadaṅgayuvatī Yogayuktā Jvālāṃśumālinī
Durāśayā Durādharṣā Durjñeyā Durgarūpiṇī | |89| |

705. Ṣaḍaṅgayuvatī
706. Yogayuktā
707. Jvālāṃśumālinī
708. Durāśayā
709. Durādharṣā
710. Durjñeyā
711. Durgarūpiṇī

Durantā Duṣkṛtiharā Durdhyeyā Duratikramā
Haṃseśvarī Trikoṇasthā
Śakambharyanukampinī | |90| |

712. Durantā
713. Duṣkṛtiharā
714. Durdhyeyā
715. Duratikramā
716. Haṃseśvarī
717. Trikoṇasthā
718. Śakambharyanukampinī

Trikoṇanilayā Nityā Paramāmṛtaraṃjitā
Mahāvidyeśvarī Śvetā Bheruṇḍā Kulasundarī | |91| |

719. Trikoṇanilayā
720. Nityā
721. Paramāmṛtaraṃjitā
722. Mahāvidyeśvarī
723. Śvetā
724. Bheruṇḍā
725. Kulasundarī

Tvaritā Bhaktisamyuktā Bhaktivaśyā Sanātanī
Bhaktānandamayī Bhaktabhāvitā
Bhaktasaṅkarī | |92| |

726. Tvaritā
727. Bhaktisaṃyuktā

बीजरूपा महामुद्रा वशिनी योगरूपिणी।
अनङ्गकुसुमाऽनङ्गमेखलाऽनङ्गरूपिणी॥86॥

(687) बीजरूपा
(688) महामुद्रा
(689) वशिनी
(690) योगरूपिणी
(691) अनङ्गकुसुमा
(692) अनङ्गमेखला
(693) अनङ्गरूपिणी

अनङ्गमदनाऽनङ्‌रेखाऽनङ्गाङ्कुशेश्वरी।
अनङ्गमालिनी कामेश्वरी सर्वार्थसाधिका॥87॥

(694) अनङ्गमदना
(695) अनङ्गरेखा
(696) अनङ्गाङ्कुशेश्वरी
(697) अनङ्गमालिनी
(698) कामेश्वरी
(699) सर्वार्थसाधिका

सर्वतंत्रमयी मोदिन्यरुणानङ्गरूपिणी।
वज्रेश्वरी च जननी सर्वदुःखाक्षयंकरी॥88॥

(700) सर्वतंत्रमयी
(701) मोदिन्यरुणानङ्गरूपिणी
(702) वज्रेश्वरी
(703) जननी
(704) सर्वदुःखक्षयंकरी

षडङ्गयुवती योगयुक्ता ज्वालांशुमालिनी।
दुराशया दुराधर्षा दुर्ज्ञेया दुर्गरूपिणी॥89॥

(705) षडङ्गयुवती
(706) योगयुक्ता
(707) ज्वालांशुमालिनी
(708) दुराशया
(709) दुराधर्षा
(710) दुर्ज्ञेया
(711) दुर्गरूपिणी

दुरन्ता दुष्कृतिहरा दुर्ध्येया दुरतिक्रमा।
हंसेश्वरी त्रिकोणस्था शाकम्भर्यनुकम्पिनी॥90॥

(712) दुरन्ता
(713) दुष्कृतिहरा
(714) दुर्ध्येया
(715) दुरतिक्रमा
(716) हंसेश्वरी
(717) त्रिकोणस्था
(718) शाकम्भर्यनुकम्पिनी

त्रिकोणनिलया नित्या परमामृतरंजिता।
महाविद्येश्वरी श्वेता भेरुण्डा कुलसुन्दरी॥91॥

(719) त्रिकोणनिलया
(720) नित्या
(721) परमामृतरंजिता
(722) महाविद्येश्वरी

728. Bhaktivaśyā
729. Sanātanī
730. Bhaktānandamayī
731. Bhaktabhāvitā
732. Bhaktaśankarī

Sarvasaundaryanilayā Sarvasaubhāgyaśālinī
Sarvasambhogabhavanī Sarvasaukhyānurupiṇī | |93| |

733. Sarvasaundaryanilayā
734. Sarvasaubhāgyaśālinī
735. Sarvasambhogabhavanī
736. Sarvasaukhyānurūpiṇī

Kumārīpujanaratā Kumārīvratachāriṇī
Kumarī Bhaktisukhinī Kumārīrūpadhāriṇī | |94| |

737. Kumārīpujanaratā
738. Kumārivratāchāriṇī
739. Kumārī
740. Bhaktisukhinī
741. Kumārirūpadhāriṇī

Kumāripūjakaprītā Kumāriprītidapriyā
Kumārīsevakāsaṃgā Kumārīsevakālayā | |95| |

742. Kumārīpūjakaprītā
743. Kumāriprītidapriyā
744. Kumārīsevakāsaṃgā
745. Kumārīsevakālayā

Ānandabhairavī Bālabhairavī Baṭubhairavī
Śmaśānabhairavī Kālabhairavī Purabhairavī | |96| |

746. Ānandabhairavī
747. Bālabhairavī
748. Baṭubhairavī
749. Śmaśanabhairavī
750. Kālabhairavī
751. Purabhairavī

Mahābhairavapatnī Cha Paramanāndabhairvī
Surānandbhairavī Cha Unmattānadabhairavī | |97| |

752. Mahābhairavapatnī
753. Paramānandabhairavī
754. Suranandabhairavī
755. Unmattānandbhairavī

Muktyānandabhairvī Cha Tathā Taruṇabhairavī
Jñanānandabhairavī Cha
Amṛtānandabhairavī | |98| |

756. Muktyānandbhairavī Tathā

(723) श्वेता (724) भेरुंडा

(725) कुलसुंदरी

त्वरिता भक्तिसंयुक्ता भक्तिवश्या सनातनी।

भक्तानन्दमयी भक्तभाविता भक्तशङ्करी॥92॥

(726) त्वरिता (727) भक्तिसंयुक्ता

(728) भक्तिवश्या (729) सनातनी

(730) भक्तानन्दमयी (731) भक्तभाविता

(732) भक्तशङ्करी

सर्वसौन्दर्यनिलया सर्वसौभाग्यशालिनी।

सर्वसम्भोगभवनी सर्वसौख्यानुरूपिणी॥93॥

(733) सर्वसौन्दर्यनिलया (734) सर्वसौभाग्यशालिनी

(735) सर्वसंभोगभवनी (736) सर्वसौख्यानुरूपिणी

कुमारीपूजनरता कुमारीव्रतचारिणी।

कुमारी भक्तिसुखिनी कुमारीरूपधारिणी॥93॥

(737) कुमारीपूजनरता (738) कुमारीव्रतचारिणी

(739) कुमारी (740) भक्तिसुखिनी

(741) कुमारीरूपधारिणी

कुमारीपूजकप्रीता कुमारीप्रीतिदप्रिया।

कुमारीसेवकासंगा कुमारीसेवकालया॥95॥

(742) कुमारीपूजकप्रीता (743) कुमारीप्रीतिदप्रिया

(744) कुमारीसेवकासंगा (745) कुमारीसेवकालया

आनन्दभैरवी बालभैरवी बटुभैरवी।

श्मशानभैरवी कालभैरवी पुरभैरवी॥96॥

(746) आनंदभैरवी (747) बालभैरवी

(748) बटुभैरवी (749) श्मशानभैरवी

(750) कालभैरवी (751) पुरभैरवी

महाभैरवपत्नी च परमानन्दभैरवी।

सुरानन्दभैरवी च उन्मत्तानन्दभैरवी॥97॥

(752) महाभैरवपत्नी (753) परमानंदभैरवी

(754) सुरानन्दभैरवी (755) उन्मत्तानंदभैरवी

757. Taruṇabhairavī
758. Jñanānandabhairavī
759. Amṛtānandabhairavī

Mahābhayaṃkarī Tīvrā Tīvravegā Tarasvinī
Tripurā Parameśānī Sundarī Purasundarī I I99I I

760. Mahābhayaṃkarī
761. Tīvrā
762. Tīvravegā
763. Tarasvinī
764. Tripurā
765. Paramesānī
766. Sundarī
767. Purasundarī

Tripureśvarī Pañchadaśī Pañchamī Puravāsinī
Mahāsaptadasī Chaiva Ṣoḍaśī Tripureśvarī I I100I I

768. Tripureśvarī
769. Pañchadaśī
770. Pañchamī
771. Puravāsinī
772. Mahāsaptadaśī Chaiva
773. Soḍaśī
774. Tripureṣvarī

Mahāṃkuśasvarūpā Cha Mahāchakreśvarī Tathā
Navachakreśvarī Chakreśvari Tripuramālinī I I101I I

775. Mahāṃkuśasvarūpā
776. Mahāchakreśvarī Tathā
777. Navachakreśvarī
778. Cakreśvarī
779. Tripuramālinī

Rājachakreśvarī Vīrā Mahātripurasundarī
Sindūrapūraruchirā Srīmattripurasundarī I I102I I

780. Rājachakreśvarī
781. Vīrā
782. Mahātripurasundarī
783. Sindūrapūraruchirā
784. Śrīmattripurasundarī

Sarvāngasundarī Raktā Raktavastrottarīyakā
Yavā Yāvakasindūraraktachandandhāriṇī I I103I I

785. Savangasundarī
786. Raktā
787. Raktavastrottarīyakā
788. Yavā

मुक्त्यानन्दभैरवी च तथा तरुणभैरवी।
ज्ञानानन्दभैरवी च अमृतानन्दभैरवी॥98॥

(756) मुक्त्यानंदभैरवी (757) तरुणभैरवी
(758) ज्ञानानंदभैरवी (759) अमृतानंदभैरवी

महाभयंकरी तीव्रा तीव्रवेगा तरस्विनी।
त्रिपुरा परमेशानी सुन्दरी पुरसुन्दरी॥99॥

(760) महाभयंकरी (761) तीव्रा
(762) तीव्रवेगा (763) तरस्विनी
(764) त्रिपुरा (765) परमेशानी
(766) सुंदरी (767) परसुंदरी

त्रिपुरेश्वरी पञ्चदशी पञ्चमी पुरवासिनी।
महासप्तदशी चैव षोडशी त्रिपुरेश्वरी॥100॥

(768) त्रिपुरेश्वरी (769) पञ्चदशी
(770) पञ्चमी (771) पुरवासिनी
(772) महासप्तदशी (773) षोडशी
(774) त्रिपुरेश्वरी

महांकुशस्वरूपा च महाचक्रेश्वरी तथा।
नवचक्रेश्वरी चक्रेश्वरी त्रिपुरमालिनी॥101॥

(775) महांकुशस्वरूपा (776) महाचक्रेश्वरी तथा
(777) नवचक्रेश्वरी (778) चक्रेश्वरी
(779) त्रिपुरमालिनी

राजचक्रेश्वरी वीरा महात्रिपुरसुन्दरी।
सिन्दूरपूररुचिरा श्रीमत्त्रिपुरसुन्दरी॥102॥

(780) राजचक्रेश्वरी (781) वीरा
(782) महात्रिपुरसुंदरी (783) सिन्दूरपूररुचिरा
(784) श्रीमत्त्रिपुरसुंदरी

सर्वाङ्गसुन्दरी रक्ता रक्तवस्त्रोत्तरीयका।
यवा यावकसिन्दूररक्तचन्दनधारिणी॥103॥

(785) सर्वाङ्गसुन्दरी (786) रक्ता
(787) रक्तवस्त्रोत्तरीयका (788) यवा
(789) यावकसिन्दूररक्तचन्दनधारिणी

789. Yāvakasindūraraktachandanadhāriṇī

Yavāyāvakasindūraraktachandanarūpadhṛk
Chamari Vāchakuṭilanirmalaśyāmakeśinī | | 104 | |

790. Yavāyāvakasindūraraktachandanarūpadhṛk
791. Chamarī
792. Vāchakuṭilanirmalaśyāmakeśinī

Vajramauktikaratnādyakirīṭamukutojjvalā
Patakundalasamvuktasphuradgandamanorama | 105 | |

793. Vajramauktikaratnādyakirīṭamukutojjvalā
794. Ratnakuṇḍalasaṃyuktasphuradgaṇḍmanoramā

Kuñjareśvarakumukbhotthamuktārañjitanāsikā
Muktāvidrūmamāṇikyahārāḍhyastanamaṇḍalā | | 106 | |

795. Kuñjareśvarakumukbhotthamuktārañjitanāsikā
796. Muktāvidrūmamāṇikyahārāḍhyastanamaṇḍalā

Sūryakāntendukāntāḍhyasparśāśmakaṇṭhabhūṣaṇā
Bijapurasphuradbījadantapaṃktiranuttamā | | 107 | |

797. Sūryakāntendukāntāḍhyasparśāśmakaṇṭhabhūṣaṇā
798. Bijapurasphuradbījadantapaṃktiranuttamā

Kāmakodaṇḍakābhugnabhrūyugākṣipravartinī
Mātangakumbhavakṣojā
Lasatkokanadekṣaṇā | | 108 | |

899. Kāmakodaṇḍakābhugnabhrūyugākṣipravartinī
800. Mātangakumbhavakṣojā
801. Lasatkokanadekṣaṇā

Manojñaśaṣkulīkarṇā Haṃsīgativiḍambinī
padmarāgāṃgadadyotaddoṡchatuṣkaprakāsinī | | 109 | |

802. Manojñaśaṣkulīkarṇā
803. Haṃsīgativiḍambinī
804. Padmarāgāṃgadadyotaddoścatuṣkaprakāsinī

Nānāmaṇiparisphūryacchuddhakāñchanakaṃkaṇā
Nāgendradantanirmānavalayāñchitapāṇikā | | 110 | |

805. Nānāmaṇiparisphūryacchuddhakāñchanakaṃkaṇā
806. Nāgendradantanirmānavalayāñchitapāṇikā

Aṃgurīyakachitraṃgī Vichitrakṣudraghantikā
Paṭṭāmbaraparīdhānā Kalamañjirarañjinī | | 111 | |

807. Aṃgurīyakachitrāṃgī
808. Vichitrakṣudraghaṇṭikā
809. Paṭṭambaraparīdhānā
810. Kalamañjīrarañjinī

Karpūrāgurukastūrīkuṃkumadravalepita
Vichitraratnaprthivikalpaśākhātalasthitā | | 112 | |

811. Karpūrāgurukastūrīkuṃkumadravalepita

यवायावकसिन्दूररक्तचन्दनरूपधृक्।
चमरी वाचकुटिलनिर्मलश्यामकेशिनी॥104

(790) यवायावकसिन्दूररक्तचन्दनरूपधृक्

(791) चमरी (792) वाचकुटिलनिर्मलश्यामकेशिनी

वज्रमौक्तिकरत्नाढ्यकिरीटमुकुटोज्ज्वला।
रत्नकुण्डलसंयुक्तस्फुरद्गण्डमनोरमा॥105॥

(793) वज्रमौक्तिकरत्नाढ्यकिरीटमुकुटोज्ज्वला

(794) रत्नकुंडलसंयुक्तस्फुरद्गंडमनोरमा

कुञ्जरेश्वरकुम्भोत्थमुक्तारञ्जितनासिका।
मुक्ताविद्रूममाणिक्यहाराढ्यस्तनमण्डला॥106॥

(795) कुञ्जरेश्वरकुम्भोत्थमुक्तारञ्जितनासिका

(796) मुक्ताविद्रूममाणिक्यहाराढ्यस्तनमंडला

सूर्यकान्तेन्दुकान्ताढ्यस्पर्शाश्मकण्ठभूषणा।
बीजपूरस्फुरद्बीजदन्तपंक्तिरनुत्तमा॥107॥

(797) सूर्यकान्तेन्दुकान्ताढ्यस्पर्शाश्मकंठभूषणा

(798) बीजपूरस्फुरद्बीजदन्तपंक्तिरनुत्तमा

कामकोदण्डकाभुग्नभ्रूयुगाक्षिप्रवर्तिनी।
मातङ्गकुम्भवक्षोजा लसत्कोकनदेक्षणा॥108॥

(799) कामकोदण्डकाभुग्नभ्रूयुगाक्षिप्रवर्तिनी

(800) मातङ्गकुम्भवक्षोजा (801) लसत्कोकनदेक्षणा

मनोज्ञशष्कुलीकर्णा हंसीगतिविडम्बिनी।
पद्मरागांगदद्योतद्दोश्चतुष्कप्रकाशिनी॥109॥

(802) मनोज्ञशष्कुलीकर्णा (803) हंसीगतिविडम्बिनी

(804) पद्मरागांगदद्योतद्दोश्चतुष्कप्रकाशिनी

नानामणिपरिस्फूर्यच्छुद्धकाञ्चनकंकणा।
नागेन्द्रदन्तनिर्माणवलयाञ्चितपाणिका॥110॥

(805) नानामणिपरिस्फूर्यच्छुद्धकाञ्चनकंकणा

(806) नागेन्द्रदन्तनिर्माणवलययाञ्चितपाणिका

अंगुरीयकचित्रांगी विचित्रक्षुद्रघण्टिका।
पट्टाम्बरपरीधाना कलमञ्जीररञ्जिनी॥111॥

(807) अंगुरीयकाचित्रांगी (808) विचित्रक्षुद्रघंटिका

(809) पट्टाम्बरपरीधाना (810) कलमञ्जीररञ्जिनी

812. Vichitraratnaprthivikalpaśākhātalasthitā

Ratnadvīpasphuradratnasiṃhāsananivāsinī
Ṣaṭcakrabhedanakarī Paramānandarūpiṇī I I 113 I I

813. Ratnadvīpasphuradratnasiṃhāsananivāsinī
814. Ṣaṭchakrabhedanakarī
815. Paramānandarūpiṇī

Sahasradalapadmāntśchandramaṇḍalavartini
Brahmarūpaśivakroḍanānāsukhavilāsinī I I 114 I I

816. Sahasradalapadmāntśchandramaṇḍalavartini
817. Brahmarūpaśivakroḍanānāsukhavilāsinī

Haraviṣṇuvirañchīndragrahanāyakasevitā
Ātmayonirbrahmayonirjagadyoniryonijā I I 115 I I

818. Haraviṣṇuvirañchīndragrahanāyakasevitā
819. Ātmayoniḥ
820. Brahmayoniḥ
821. Jagadyoniḥ
822. Ayonijā

Bhagarūpā Bhagasthatri Bhaginībhagadhāriṇī
Bhagātmikā Bhagādhārarūpiṇī Bhagaśālinī I I 116 I I

823. Bhagarūpā
824. Bhagasthātrī
825. Bhaginibhagadhāriṇī
826. Bhagātmikā
827. Bhagādhārarūpiṇī
828. Bhagaśālinī

Lingābhidhāyinī Lingapriyālinganivāsinī
Lingasthā Linginī Lingarūpiṇī Lingasundarī I I 117 I I

829. Lingābhidhāyinī
830. Lingapriyā
831. Linganivāsinī
832. Lingasthā
833. Linginī
834. Lingarūpiṇī
835. Lingasundarī

Lingagītimahāprītir Bhagagītirmahāsukhā
Linganāmasadānandā Bhaganāmasadāratiḥ I I 118 I I

836. Lingagītimahāprītiḥ
837. Bhagagītirmahāsukhā
838, Linganāmasadānadā
839. Bhaganāmasadāratiḥ

कर्पूरागुरुकस्तूरीकुंकुमद्रवलेपिता।
विचित्ररत्नपृथिवीकल्पशाखातलस्थिता॥112॥

(811) कर्पूरागुरुकस्तूरीकुंकुमद्रवलेपिता

(812) विचित्ररत्नपृथिवीकल्पशाखातलस्थिता

रत्नद्वीपस्फुरद्रत्नसिंहासननिवासिनी।
षट्चक्रभेदनकरी परमानन्दरूपिणी॥113॥

(813) रत्नद्वीपस्फुरद्रत्नसिंहासननिवासिनी

(814) षट्चक्रभेदनकरी (815) परमानंदरूपिणी

सहस्रदल-पद्मान्तश्चन्द्र-मण्डलवर्तिनी।
ब्रह्मरूप-शिवक्रोड-नानासुखविलासिनी॥114॥

(816) सहस्रदलपद्मान्तश्चन्द्रमंडलवर्तिनी

(817) ब्रह्मरूपशिवक्रोडनानासुखविलासिनी

हरविष्णुविरञ्चीन्द्रग्रहनायकसेविता।
आत्मयोनिर्ब्रह्मयोनिर्जगद्योनिरयोनिजा॥115॥

(818) हरविष्णुविरञ्चीन्द्रग्रहनायकसेविता

(819) आत्मयोनि (820) ब्रह्मयोनि

(821) जगद्योनि (822) अयोनिजा

भगरूपा भगस्थात्री भगिनीभगधारिणी।
भगात्मिका भगाधाररूपिणी भगशालिनी॥116॥

(823) भगरूपा (824) भगस्थात्री

(825) भगिनीभगधारिणी (826) भगात्मिका

(827) भगाधाररूपिणी (828) भगशालिनी

लिङ्गाभिधायिनी लिङ्गप्रियालिङ्गनिवासिनी।
लिङ्गस्था लिङ्गिनी लिङ्गरूपिणी लिङ्गसुन्दरी॥117॥

(829) लिङ्गाभिधायिनी (830) लिङ्गप्रिया

(831) लिङ्गनिवासिनी (832) लिङ्गस्था

(833) लिङ्गिनी (834) लिङ्गरूपिणी

(835) लिङ्गसुन्दरी

लिङ्गगीतिमहाप्रीतिर्भगगीतिर्महासुखा।
लिङ्गनामसदानन्दा भगनामसदारतिः॥118॥

(836) लिङ्गगीतिमहाप्रीति (837) भगगीतिर्महासुखा

(838) लिङ्गनामसदानन्दा (839) भगनामसदारति

Bhaganāmasadānadā Linganāmasadāratiḥ
Lingamālākaṇṭhabhūṣā
Bhagamālāvibhūṣaṇā I I 119 I I

840. Bhaganāmasādānadā
841. Linganāmasadāratiḥ
842. Lingamālākaṇṭhabhūṣā
843. Bhagamālāvibhūṣaṇā

Bhagalingāmṛtprītā Bhagalingāmṛtātmikā
Bhagalingārchanaprītā Bhagalingaśvarūpiṇī I I 120 I I

844. Bhagalingāmṛtprītā
845. Bhagalingāmṛtātmikā
846, Bhagalingārchanaprītā
847. Bhagalingaśvarūpiṇī

Bhaglingasvarūpā Cha Bhagalingasukhāvahā
Svayambhūkusumaprītā
Svayambhūkusumārcitā I I 121 I I

848. Bhagalingasvarūpā
849. Bhagalingasukhāvahā
850. Svayambhūkusumaprītā
851. Svayambhūkusumārchitā

Svayambhūkusumaprāṇā Svayambhūkusumotthitā
Svayambhūkusumasnātā
Svayambhūpuṣpatarpitā I I 122 I I

852. Svayambhūkusumaprāṇā
853. Svayambhūkusumotthitā
854. Svayambhūkusumasnātā
855. Svayambhūpuṣpatarpitā

Svayambhūpuṣpaghaṭitā Svayambhūpuṣpadhāriṇī
Svayambhūpuṣpatilakā
Svayambhūpuṣpacharchitā I I 123 I I

856. Svayambhupuṣpaghaṭitā
857. Svayambhūpuṣpadhāriṇī
858. Svayambhūpuṣpatilkā
859. Svayambhūpuṣpacharchitā

Svayambhūpuṣpaniratā Svayambhūkusumagrahā
Svayambhūpuṣayajñāmgā
Svayambhūkusumātmikā I I 124 I I

860. Svayambhūpuṣpaniratā
861. Svayambhūkusumagrahā
862. Svayambhūpuṣpayajñamgā
863. Svayambhūkusumātmikā

भगनामसदानन्दा लिङ्गनामसदारतिः।
लिङ्गमालाकण्ठभूषा भगमालाविभूषणा॥119॥

(840) भगनामसदानंदा (841) लिङ्गनामसदारति
(842) लिङ्गमालाकण्ठभूषा (843) भगमालाविभूषणा

भगलिंगामृतप्रीता भगलिंगामृतात्मिका।
भगलिंगार्चनप्रीता भगलिङ्गस्वरूपिणी॥120॥

(844) भगलिंगामृतप्रीता (845) भगलिंगामृतात्मिका
(846) भगलिंगार्चनप्रीता (847) भगलिङ्गस्वरूपिणी

भगलिङ्गस्वरूपा च भगलिङ्गसुखावहा।
स्वयम्भूकुसुमप्रीता स्वयम्भूकुसुमार्चिता॥121॥

(848) भगलिङ्गस्वरूपा (849) भगलिङ्गसुखावहा
(850) स्वयम्भूकुसुमप्रीता (851) स्वयम्भूकुसुमार्चिता

स्वयम्भूकुसुमप्राणा स्वयम्भूकुसुमोत्थिता।
स्वयम्भूकुसुमस्नाता स्वयम्भूपुष्पतर्पिता॥122॥

(852) स्वयम्भूकुसुमप्राणा (853) स्वयम्भूकुसुमोत्थिता
(854) स्वयम्भूकुसुमस्नाता (855) स्वयभूपुष्पतर्पिता

स्वयम्भूपुष्पघटिता स्वयम्भूपुष्पधारिणी।
स्वयम्भूपुष्पतिलका स्वयम्भूपुष्पचर्चिता॥123॥

(856) स्वयम्भूपुष्पघटिता (857) स्वयम्भूपुष्पधारिणी
(858) स्वयम्भूपुष्पतिलका (859) स्वयम्भूपुष्पचर्चिता

स्वयम्भूपुष्पनिरता स्वयम्भूकुसुमग्रहा।
स्वयम्भूपुष्पयज्ञांगा स्वयम्भूकुसुमात्मिका॥124॥

(860) स्वयम्भूपुष्पनिरता (861) स्वयम्भूकुसुमग्रहा
(862) स्वयम्भूपुष्पयज्ञांगा (863) स्वयम्भूकुसुमात्मिका

स्वयम्भूपुष्परचिता स्वयम्भूकुसुमप्रिया।
स्वयम्भूकुसुमादानलालसोन्मत्तमानसा॥125॥

(864) स्वयम्भूपुष्परचिता (865) स्वयम्भूकुसुमप्रिया
(866) स्वयम्भूकुसुमादानलालसोन्मत्तमानसा

स्वयम्भूकुसुमानन्दलहरीस्निग्धदेहिनी।
स्वयम्भूकुसुमधारा स्वयम्भूकुसुमाकुला॥126॥

(867) स्वयम्भूकुसुमानन्दलहरीस्निग्धदेहिनी
(868) स्वयम्भूकुसुमधारा (869) स्वयम्भूकुसुमाकुला

Svayambhūpuṣparachitā Svayambhūkusumapriyā
Svayambhūkusumādānalalāsonmattamānasā I I 125 I I

864. Svayambhūpuṣparachitā
865. Svayambhūkusumapriyā
866. Svayambhūkusumādānalālāsonmattamānasā

Svayambhūkusumānandalaharīsnigdhadehinī
Svayambhūkusumadhārā
Svayambhūkusumākulā I I 126 I I

867, Svaymbhūkusumānandalaharīsnigdhadehinī
868, Svayambhūkusumadhārā
869. Svayambhūkusumākulā

Svayambhūpuṣpanilyā Svayambhūpuspavāsinī
Svayambhūkusumasnigdhā
Svayambhūkusumotsukā I I 127 I I

870. Svayambhūpuṣpanilayā
871. Svayambhūpuṣpavāsinī
872. Svayambhūkusumasnigdhā
873. Svayambhūkusumotsukā

Svayambhūpuṣpakāriṇī Svayambhūpuṣpapālikā
Svayambhukusumadhyānā
Svayambhūkusumaprabhā I I 128 I I

874. Svayambhūpuṣpakāriṇī
875. Svayambhūpuṣpapālikā
876. Svayambhūkusumadhyānā
877. Svayambhūkusumaprabhā

Svayambhūkusumajñānā Svayambhūpuspabhogiṇi
Svayambhūkusumānandā
Svayambhūpuṣpavarṣinī I I 129 I I

878, Svayambhūkusumajñanā
879. Svayambhūpuṣpabhogiṇī
880. Svayambhūkusumānandā
881. Svayambhūpuṣpavarṣiṇī

Svayambhūkusumotsāhā Svayambhūpuspapuṣpiṇī
Svayambhūkusumotsaṃgā
Svayambhūpuṣparūpiṇī I I 130 I I

882. Svayambhūkusumotsahā
883. Svayambhūpuṣpapuṣpiṇī
884. Svayambhūkusumotsaṃgā
885. Svayambhūpuṣparūpiṇī

स्वयम्भूपुष्पनिलया स्वयम्भूपुष्पवासिनी।
स्वयम्भूकुसुमस्निग्धा स्वयम्भूकुसुमोत्सुका॥127॥

(870) स्वयम्भूपुष्पनिलया (871) स्वयम्भूपुष्पवासिनी
(872) स्वयम्भूकुसुमस्निग्धा (873) स्वयम्भूकुसुमोत्सुका

स्वयम्भूपुष्पकारिणी स्वयम्भूपुष्पपालिका।
स्वयम्भूकुसुमध्याना स्वयमभूकुसुमप्रभा॥128॥

(874) स्वयम्भूपुष्पकारिणी (875) स्वयम्भूपुष्पपालिका
(876) स्वयम्भूकुसुमध्याना (877) स्वयमभूकुसुमप्रभा

स्वयम्भूकुसुमज्ञाना स्वयम्भूपुष्पभोगिणी।
स्वयम्भूकुसुमानन्दा स्वयम्भूपुष्पवर्षिणी॥129॥

(878) स्वयम्भूकुसुमज्ञाना (879) स्वयम्भूपुष्पभोगिणी
(880) स्वयम्भूकुसुमानन्दा (881) स्वयम्भूपुष्पवर्षिणी

स्वयम्भूकुसुमोत्साहा स्वयम्भूपुष्पपुष्पिणी।
स्वयम्भूकुसुमोत्संगा स्वयम्भूपुष्परूपिणी॥130॥

(882) स्वयम्भूकुसुमोत्साहा (883) स्वयम्भूपुष्पपुष्पिणी
(884) स्वयम्भूकुसुमोत्संगा (885) स्वयम्भूपुष्परूपिणी

स्वयम्भूकुसुमोन्मादा स्वयम्भूपुष्पसुन्दरी।
स्वयम्भूकुसुमाराध्या स्वयम्भूकुसुमोद्भवा॥131॥

(886) स्वयम्भूकुसुमोन्मादा (887) स्वयम्भूपुष्पसुन्दरी
(888) स्वयम्भूकुसुमाराध्या (889) स्वयम्भूकुसुमोद्भवा

स्वयम्भूकुसुमव्यग्रा स्वयम्भूपुष्पवर्णिता।
स्वयम्भूपूजकप्रज्ञा स्वयम्भूहोतृमातृका॥132॥

(890) स्वयंभूकुसुमव्यग्रा (891) स्वयंभूपुष्पवर्णिता
(892) स्वयंभूपूजकप्रज्ञा (893) स्वयंभूहोतृमातृका

स्वयम्भूदातृरक्षित्री स्वयम्भूभक्तभाविका।
स्वयम्भूकुसुमप्रज्ञा स्वयम्भूपूजकप्रिया॥133॥

(894) स्वयंभूदातृरक्षित्री (895) स्वयंभूभक्तभाविका
(896) स्वयंभूकुसुमप्रज्ञा (897) स्वयंभूपूजकप्रिया

स्वयम्भूवन्दकाधारा स्वयम्भूनिन्दकान्तका।
स्वयम्भूप्रदसर्वस्वा स्वयम्भूदरूपिणी॥134॥

(898) स्वयंभूवन्दकाधारा (899) स्वयंभूनिन्दकान्तका
(900) स्वयंभूप्रदसर्वस्वा (901) स्वयंभूदरूपिणी

Svayambhūkusumonmādā Svayambhūpuṣpasundarī
S v a y a m b h ¯u k u s u m ¯a r ¯a d h y ¯a
Svayambhūkusumodbhavā I I 131 I I

886. Svayambhūkusumonmādā
887. Svayambhūpuṣpasundarī
888. Svayambhūkusumārādhyā
889. Svayambhūkusumodbhavā

Svayambhūkusumavyagrā Svayambhūpuṣpavarnitā
Svayambhūpujakaprajñā
Svayambhūhotṛmātṛkā I I 132 I I

890. Svayambhūkusumavyagrā
891. Svayambhūpuṣpavarṃitā
892. Svayambhūpūjakaprajñā
893. Svayambhūhotṛmātṛkā

Svayambhūdātṛrakṣitrī Svayambhūbhaktabhāvikā
Svayambhūkusumaprajñā
Svayambhūpūjakapriyā I I 133 I I

894. Svaymbhūdātṛrakṣitrī
895. Svayambhūbhaktabhāvikā
896. Svayambhūkusumaprajñā
897. Svayambhūpūjakapriyā

Svayambhūvandakādhārā Svayambhūnindakāntakā
Svayambhūpradasarvasvā
Svayambhūpradarūpiṇī I I 134 I I

898. Svayambhūvandakādhārā
899. Svayambhūnindakāntakā
900. Svayambhūpradasarvasvā
901. Svayambhūpradarūpiṇī

Svayambhūpradasasmerā Svayambharddhaśarīriṇī
Sarvakālodbhavaprītā
Sarvakālodbhavātmīkā I I 135 I I

902. Svayambhūpradasasmerā
903. Svayambharddhaśarīriṇī
904. Sarvakālodbhavaprītā
905. Sarvakālodbhavātmīkā

Sarvakālodbhavodbhāvā Sarvakālodbhavodbhavā
Kuṇḍapuṣpasadāprītirgolapuṣpasadāgatiḥ I I 136 I I

906. Sarvakālodbhavodbhāvā
907. Sarvakālodbhavodbhavā
908. Kuṇḍapuṣpasadāprītiḥ
909. Golapuṣpasadāgatiḥ

स्वयम्भूप्रदसस्मेरा स्वयम्भूदर्धशरीरिणी।
सर्वकालोद्भवप्रीता सर्वकालोध्वात्मिका॥135॥

(902) स्वयंभूप्रदसस्मेरा (903) स्वयंभूदर्धशरीरिणी
(904) सर्वकालोद्भवप्रीता (905) सर्वकालोर्ध्वात्मिका

सर्वकालोद्भवोद्भवा सर्वकालोद्भवोद्भवा।
कुण्डपुष्पसदाप्रीतिर्गोलपुष्पसदागतिः॥136॥

(906) सर्वकालोद्भवोद्भावा (907) सर्वकालोद्भवोद्भवा
(908) कुंडपुष्पसदाप्रीति (909) गोलापुष्पसदागति

कुण्डगोलोद्भवप्रीता कुण्डगोलोद्भवात्मिका।
शुक्रधारा शुक्ररूपा शुक्रसिन्धुनिवासिनी॥137॥

(910) कुंडगोलोद्भवप्रीता (911) कुंडगोलोद्भवात्मिका
(912) शुक्रधारा (913) शुक्ररूपा
(914) शुक्रसिंधुनिवासिनी

शुक्रालया शुक्रभोगा शुक्रपूजासदारतिः।
रक्ताशया रक्तभोगा रक्तपूजासदारतिः॥138॥

(915) शुक्रालया (916) शुक्रभोगा
(917) शुक्रपूजासदारति (918) रक्ताशया
(919) रक्तभोगा (920) रक्तपूजासदारति

रक्तपूजारक्तहोमा रक्तस्था रक्तवत्सला।
रक्तवर्णा रक्तदेहा रक्तपूजकपुत्रिणी॥139॥

(921) रक्तपूजा (922) रक्तहोमा
(923) रक्तस्था (924) रक्तवत्सला
(925) रक्तवर्णा (926) रक्तदेहा
(927) रक्तपूजकपुत्रिणी

रक्तद्युति रक्तस्पृहा देवी च रक्तसुन्दरी।
रक्ताभिधेया रक्तार्हा रक्तकन्दरवन्दिता॥140॥

(928) रक्तद्युति (929) रक्तस्पृहा
(930) देवी (931) रक्तसुन्दरी
(932) रक्ताभिधेया (933) रक्तार्हा
(934) रक्तकन्दरवन्दिता

Kuṇḍagolodbhavaprītā Kuṇḍagolodbhavātmikā
Śukradhārā Śukrarūpā Śukrasindhunivāsinī | | 137 | |

910. Kuṇḍagolodbhavaprītā
911. Kuṇḍagolodbhavātmikā
912. Śukradhārā
913. Śukrarūpā
914. Śukrasindhunivāsinī

Śukrālayā Śukrabhogā Śukrapūjāsadāratiḥ
Raktasayā Raktabhogā Raktapūjāsadāratiḥ | | 138 | |

915. Śukrālayā
916. Śukrabhogā
917. Śukrapūjāsadāratiḥ
918. Raktāśayā
919. Raktabhogā
920. Raktapūjāsadāratiḥ

Raktapūjāraktahomā Raktasthā Raktavatsalā
Raktavarṇā Ratkadehā Raktapūjakaputriṇī | | 139 | |

921. Raktapūjā
922. Raktahomā
923. Raktasthā
924. Raktavatsalā
925. Raktavarṇā
926. Raktadehā
927. Raktapūjakaputriṇī

Raktadyutī Raktaspṛhā Devī Cha Raktasundarī
Raktābhidheyā Raktārhā
Raktakandaravanditā | | 140 | |

928. Raktadyutī
929. Raktaspṛhā
930. Devī
931. Raktasundarī
932. Raktābhidheyā
933. Raktārhā
934. Raktakandaravanditā

Mahāraktā Raktabhavā Raktasṛṣṭividhāyinī
Raktasnātā Raktasiktā Raktasevyātiraktini | | 141 | |

935. Mahāraktā
936. Raktabhavā
937. Raktasṛṣṭividhāyinī
938, Raktasnātā
939. Raktasiktā
940. Raktasevyātiraktinī

महारक्ता रक्तभवा रक्तसृष्टिविधायिनी।
रक्तस्नाता रक्तसिक्ता रक्तसेव्यातिरक्तिनी॥141॥

(935) महारक्ता (936) रक्तभवा
(937) रक्तसृष्टिविधायिनी (938) रक्तस्नाता
(939) रक्तसिक्ता (940) रक्तसेव्यातिरक्तिनी

रक्तानन्दकरी रक्तसदानन्दविधायिनी।
रक्ताशया रक्तपूर्णा रक्तसेव्या मनोरमा॥142॥

(941) रक्तानंदकरी (942) रक्तसदानन्दविधायिनी
(943) रक्ताशया (944) रक्तपूर्णा
(945) रक्तसेव्या (946) मनोरमा

रक्तपूजकसर्वस्वा रक्तनिन्दकनाशिनी।
रक्तात्मिका रक्तरूपा रक्ताकर्षणकारिणी॥143॥

(947) रक्तपूजकसर्वस्वा (948) रक्तनिन्दकनाशिनी
(949) रक्तात्मिका (950) रक्तरूपा
(951) रक्ताकर्षणकारिणी

रक्तोत्साहा च रक्ताढया रक्तपानपरायणा।
शोणितानन्दजननी कल्लोलस्निग्धरूपिणी॥144॥

(952) रक्तोत्साहा (953) रक्ताढ्या
(954) रक्तपानपरायणा (955) शोणितानंदजननी
(956) कल्लोलस्निग्धरूपिणी

साधकान्तर्गता देवी पायिनी पापनाशिनी।
साधकानां सुखकरी साधकारिविनाशिनी॥145॥

(957) साधकांतर्गता देवी (958) पायिनी
(959) पापनाशिनी (960) साधकानां सुखकरी
(961) साधकारिविनाशिनी

साधकानां हृदिस्थात्री साधकानन्दकारिणी।
साधकानाञ्च जननी साधकप्रियकारिणी॥146॥

(962) साधकानां हृदिस्थात्री (963) साधकानंदकारिणी
(964) साधकानाञ्च जननी (965) साधकप्रियकारिणी

साधकप्रचुरानन्दसम्पत्तिसुखदायिनी।
शुक्रपूज्या शुक्रहोमसन्तुष्टा शुक्रवत्सला॥147॥

(966) साधकप्रचुरानन्दसम्पत्तिसुखदायिनी

Raktānandakarī Raktasadānandavidhāyinī
Raktāsayā Raktapūrṇā Raktasevyā
Manoramā॥142॥

941.Raktānandakarī
942. Raktasadānandavidhāyinī
943. Raktāśayā
944. Raktapūrṇā
945. Raktasevyā
946. Manoramā

Raktapūjakasarvasvā Raktanindakanāśinī
Raktātmikā Raktarūpā Raktākarṣaṇakāriṇī॥143॥

947. Raktapūjakasarvasvā
948. Raktanindakanāśinī
949. Raktātmikā
950. Raktarūpā
951. Raktākarṣaṇakāriṇī

Raktotsāhā cha Raktāḍhyā Raktapānaparāyaṇā
Soṇitānandanjananī Kallolasnigdharūpiṇī॥144॥

952. Raktotsāhā
953. Radtāḍhyā
954. Raktapānaparāyaṇā
955. Śoṇitānandjananī
956. Kallolasnigdharūpiṇī

Sādhakāntargatā Devī Pāyinī Pāpanāśinī
Sāchakānāṃ Sukhakarī Sadhakārivināśinī॥145॥

957. Sādhakāntargatā Devī
958. Pāyinī
959. Pāpanāśinī
960. Sāchakānāṃ Sukhakarī
961. Sadhakārivināśinī

Sādhakānām Hṛdisthātrī Sādhakānandakāriṇī
Sadhakānāñcha Jananī Sadhakapriyakāriṇī॥146॥

962. Sādhakānām Hṛdisthātrī
963. Sādhakānandakāriṇī
964. Sadhakānāñcha Jananī
965. Sadhakapriyakāriṇī

Sādhakapracurānandasampattisukhadāyinī
Śukrapūjyā Sukrahomasantuṣṭā Śukravatsalā॥147॥

966. Sādhakaprachurānandasampattisukhādayinī
967. Sukrapūjyā
968. Śukrahomasantuṣṭā
969. Śukravatsalā

(967) शुक्रपूज्या (968) शुक्रहोमसंतुष्टा

(969) शुक्रवत्सला

शुक्रमूर्तिः शुक्रदेहा शुक्रपूजकपुत्रिणी।
शुक्रस्था शुक्रिणी शुक्रसंस्पृहा शुक्रसुन्दरी॥148॥

(970) शुक्रमूर्ति (971) शुक्रदेहा

(972) शुक्रपूजकपुत्रिणी (973) शुक्रस्था

(974) शुक्रिणी (975) शुक्रसंस्पृहा

(976) शुक्रसुंदरी

शुक्रस्नाता शुक्रकरी शुक्रसेव्यातिशुक्रिणी।
महाशुक्रा शुक्रभवा शुकवृष्टिविधायिनी॥149॥

(977) शुक्रस्नाता (978) शुक्रकरी

(979) शुक्रसेव्यातिशुक्रिणी (980) महाशुक्रा

(981) शुक्रभवा (982) शुक्रवृष्टिविधायिनी

शुक्राभिधेया शुक्रार्हाशुक्रवन्दकवन्दिता।
शुक्रानन्दकरी शुक्रसदानन्दविधायिनी॥150॥

(983) शुक्राभिधेया (984) शुक्रार्हाशुक्रवन्दकवन्दिता

(985) शुक्रानन्दकरी (986) शुक्रसदानन्दविधायिनी

शुक्रोत्सवा सदाशुक्रपूर्णा शुक्रमनोरमा।
शुक्रपूजकसर्वस्वा शुक्रनिन्दकनाशिनी॥151॥

(987) शुक्रोत्सवा (988) सदाशुक्रपूर्णा

(989) शुक्रमनोरमा (990) शुक्रपूजकसर्वस्वा

(991) शुक्रनिन्दकनाशिनी

शुक्रात्मिका शुक्रसम्पच्छुक्राकर्षकारिणी।
सारदा साधकप्राणा साधकासक्तमानसा॥152॥

(992) शुक्रात्मिका (993) शुक्रसम्पच्छुक्राकर्षकारिणी

(994) सारदा (995) साधकप्राणा

(996) साधकासक्तमानसा

साधकोत्तमसर्वस्वसाधिका भक्तवत्सला।
साधकानन्दसन्तोषा साधकाधिविनाशिनी॥153॥

(997) साधकोत्तमसर्वस्वसाधिका (998) भक्तवत्सला

(999) साधकानन्दसन्तोषा (1000) साधकाधिविनाशिनी

Śukramūrtiḥ Śukradehā Śukrapūjakaputriṇī
Śukrasthā Sukriṇi Śukrsaṃspṛhā
Śukrasundarī I I 148 I I

970. Śukramūrtiḥ 971. Śukradehā
972. Śukrapūjakaputriṇī
973. Śukrasthā
974. Śukrinī
975. Śukrasaṃsprhā
976. Śukrasundarī

Śukrasanātā Śukrakarī Śukrasevyātiśukriṇī
Mahāsukrā Śukrabhavā-Śukravrstividhāyinī I I 149 I I

977. Śukrasnātā
978. Śukrakarī
979. Śukrasevyātiśukriṇī
980. Mahāśukrā
981. Śukrabhavā
982. Śukravṛṣṭividhāyinī

Śukrābhidheyā śukrārhāśukravandakavanditā
Śukrānandakarī śukrasadānandavidhāyinī I I 150 I I

983. Śukrābhidheyā
984. Śukrārhaśukravandakavanditā
985. Śukrānandakarī
986. Śukrasadānandavidhāyinī.

Śukrotsavā Sadāśukrapūrṇā Śukramanoramā
Śukrapūjakasarvasvā Śukranindakanāśinī I I 151 I I

987. Śukrotsavā
988. Sadāśukrapūrṇā
989. Śukramanoramā
990. Śukrapūjakasarvasvā
991. Śukranindakanāśinī

Śukrātmikā Śukrasampacchukrākarṣakāriṇī
Sāradā Sādhakaprāṇā Sādhakāsaktamānasā I I 152 I I

992. Śukrātmikā
993. Śukrasampacchukrākarṣakāriṇī
994. Sarada 995. Sadhakaprana
996. Sādhakāsaktamanasā

Sādhakottamasarvasvasādhikā Bhaktavatsalā
Sādhakānandasantoṣā Sādhadakhivināsinī I I 153 I I

997. Sādhakottamasarvasvasādhikā
998. Bhaktavatsalā
999. Sādhakānandasantoṣā
1000. Sadhakādhivināśinī

आत्मविद्या ब्रह्मविद्या परब्रह्मस्वरूपिणी।
त्रिकूटस्था पंचकूटा सर्वकूटशरीरिणी।
सर्ववर्णमयी वर्णजपमालाविधायिनी॥154॥

(1001) आत्मविद्या (1002) ब्रह्मविद्या
(1003) परब्रह्मस्वरूपिणी (1004) त्रिकूटस्था
(1005) पंचकूटा (1006) सर्वकूटशरीरिणी
(1007) सर्ववर्णमयी (1008) वर्णजपमालाविधायिनी

स्फुरित मणि राणाकार प्रताने।
तारागण तू व्योम विताने॥

श्री राधा संतन हितकारिणी।
अग्निनपनि अतिदुष्ट विदारिणी॥
धूम्रविलोचन प्राणविमोचनि।
शुम्भ-निशुम्भमथनि बरलोचनि॥

सहस्त्रभुजी सरोरुह मालिनी।
चामुण्डे मरघट के वासिनी॥

खप्परमध्य सुशोणित साजी।
मारेउ मां महिषासुर पाजी॥
अम्ब अम्बिका चंड चंडिका।
सब एके तुम आदि कालिका॥

अजा एक रूपा बहु रूपा।
अकथ चरित्रा शक्ति अनूपा॥

कलकत्ते के दक्षिण द्वारे।
मूरति तोर महेश अपारे॥

कादम्बरी पानरत श्यामा।
जय मातंगि काम के धामा॥

**Ātmavidyā Brahmavidyā Parabrahmasvarūpiṇī
Trikūṭasthā Paṃchakūtā Sarvakūṭaśaririṇī
Sarvavarṇamayī Varṇājapamālāvidhāyinī I I 154 I I**

1001. Ātmavidyā
1002. Brahmavidyā
1003. Parabrahmasvarūpiṇī
1004. Trikūṭasthā
1005. Paṃchakūṭā
1006. Sarvakūṭaśarīriṇī
1007. Sarvavarnamayi
1008. Varnajapamalavidhayini

**Sfurit Mani Ranakar Pratane.
Taragan Tu Vayom Vitane.**

**Shri Radha Santan Hitkarihi,
Aganinpani Atidusht Vidarini.**

**Dhumravilochan Pranvimochani
Shumbh Nishushumbhmathani Barlochini**

**Shahastrabhuji Saroruh Malini
Chamunde Marghat Ke Vasani**

**Khapparmadhya Shushanit Shagi
Mareu maa Mahishasur Pagi**

**Amb Ambika Chand Candika
Sub Eake Tum Aadi Kalika**

**Aja ek Rupa Bahu Rupa
Aekath Charitra Shakati Anoopa**

**Kakate Ke Dakshni Dware
Moorati Tore Mahesh Apare**

**Kadambari Panrat Shyama
Jai Matangi Kaam ke Dhaama**

**Kamalasan Vashani Kamalanayani
Jaishyam Jai Jai Shyamayani**

कमलासन वासनि कमलायनि।
जयश्याम जय जय श्यामायनि॥

रासरते नवरसे प्रकृति हे।
जयति भक्त डर कुमति सुमति हरे॥

कोटिब्रह्म-शिव विष्णु कर्मदा।
जयति अहिंसा धर्म जन्मदा॥

जल-थल नभमंडल में व्यापिनी।
सौदामिनी मध्य अलापिनी॥
झननन तच्छुमरिन रिननादिनि।
जय सरस्वती वीणावादिनी॥

ऊँ ऐं ह्रीं क्लीं चामुण्डायै।
कलित गले कोमल रुण्डायै॥

जय ब्रह्मांड सिद्धकवि माता।
कामाख्या ओ काली माता॥

हिंगलाज विन्ध्यांचल वासिनी।
अट्टहासिनी अधनाशिनी॥

कितनी स्तुति करो अखंडे।
तु ब्रह्माण्ड शक्ति जितखंडे॥

□□□

Rasrate Naverashy Prakiti Hey
Jayanti Bhakat Dar Kumati Sumati Hare.

Kotibrahama - Shiv Vishnu Karmada
Jayati Ahimsha Dharma Jammmada

Jal Thal Nabhmandal Mey Vyapini
Sandamini Madhoya Alapini

Kehanam Tachumarin Rinanadini
Jai Saraswati Veenavadini

Aum Aey Hin Kleen Chamunday
Kalit Galey Komal Runday
Jai Brahmand Sidhikavi Mata
Kamakhaya oh Kali Mata

Hinglag Vindhayanchal Vashini
Athaslini Adhanashini

Kitani Stuti Karo Akhaandy
Tu Brahmamand Shakti Jeetkhand.

❑❑❑

श्रीमहाकाली क्षमापान स्तोत्र

अण्देहस्थीय दाहं तव चरण युगान्नश्रितो नार्च्चितोहम्।
तेनाद्या कीर्ति वर्ग्गेर्ज्जठरजदहने बद्धियमानो बलिष्ठैः॥
शिप्त्वाजन्मान्वरान्नः पुनरिहभविता क्वाश्रवः क्वापि सेवा।
क्षन्तव्यो मेपराधः प्रकटित वदने कामरूपे कराले॥

वाल्येवालाभिलायैर्ज्जडित जडमतिर्बाललीला प्रसक्तो।
नत्वां जानामि मातः कलिकलुषहरा भोग मोक्ष प्रदात्रीम्॥
नाचारो नैव पूजा न च यजन कथा न स्मृतिर्नैव सेवा।
क्षन्तव्योमेपराधः प्रकटित वदने कामरूपे कराले॥

प्राप्तोहं यौवनञ्चे द्विषधर सदृयैरिन्द्रियैर्दृष्ट गात्री।
नष्ट प्रज्ञः परस्त्री परधन हरणे सर्व्वदा साभिलाषः॥
त्वत्पादम्भोज युग्मङ् क्षणमपि मनसा न स्मृतोहं कदापि।
क्षन्तव्योमेपराधः प्रकटित वदने कामरूपे कराले॥

प्रौढोभिक्षाभिलाषी सुत दुहितृ कलत्रार्थमन्नादि चेष्ट।
क्व प्राप्स्ये कुत्रयामीत्यनुदिन मनिशञ्चिन्तयाग्न देहः॥
नोतेष्यानन्त चास्था न च भजन विधिन्नामा संकीर्तनं व्वा।
क्षन्तव्यो मेपराधः प्रकटित वदने कामरूपे कराले॥

वृद्धत्वे बुद्धिहीनः कृश विवशतनुश्श्वासकासातिसारैः।
कर्म्मानर्हो ऽक्षिहीनः प्रगलित दशनः क्षुत्पिपासाभिभूतः॥
पश्चातपेनदग्धो मरण मनुदिनन्ध्येय मायन्नवान्यत्।
क्षन्तव्यो मेऽपराधः प्रकटित वदने कामरूपे कराले॥

कृत्वास्नानं दिनादौ क्वचिदपि सलिलं नोकृत नैव पुष्प।
न्ते नैवेद्यदिकञ्च क्वचिदपि न कृतं नापिभावोन भक्तिः॥
वस्यासी नैव पूजा न च गुण कथनं नापि चार्च्चाकृतोत।
क्षन्तव्यो मेपराधं प्रकटित वदने कामरूपे कराले॥

Mahakali Kshamaapan Strotra

(An Apology to Goddess Mahakali)

Andehastheeya Daaham Jab Charan Yugaannshirito Naar Chittoham
Tenadya Keerti Vaggerjjrathar Jadamane Buddhiya Mano Balishtheih
Shiptwaa Janmanvarannah Punarihabhavita Kwashrayah Kwaapi Seva
Kshantasyo Meparaadhah Prakatit Vadane Kaamroope Karaale I

Balye Valaabhilanyjjadija Jadmatirbaal Leela Prasakto
Natwam Janami Matah Kali Kalushhara Bhog Mokha Pradatreem I
Nachaaro Neiva Pooja Na Cha Yajan Katha Na Smritinairvd Sewa
Kshantavyomeparaadhah Prakatit Vadane Kaamroope Karaale I

Praptoham Yauvananche Dwishadhar Sadreryerindriyeidrishta Gaatri
Nashta Pragyah Parastree Paradhan Harone Sarvada Saabhilaashah
Twatpadambhoja Yugmam Kshanamapi Manosa Na Smirtoham Kadaapi
Kshantavyome Paraadhah . . .

Vriddhatve Buddhiheenahj Krish Vivasha Tanu Shshwaas Kaasi Tsaareih
Karmmanahro-A Khihee Nah Pragalita Dashanah Khutpi Paasabhi Bhooiaj
Pashchaat Penadagdhau Maran Manudinn Dhyeya Maayannvvaan Yat
Kshanta Vyo Me Paraadham . . .
Kritvaasnaanam Dinaadi Kwachidap Salilam Nokrita Naiva Pushp I

जानामि त्वां न चाहं भवभयहरणीं सर्व्व सिद्धि प्रदात्रीम्।
न्निव्यानन्दोदयाढ्यात्यितय गुणमयीन्निय शुद्धोदयाढ्याम्॥
मिथ्या कर्म्माभिलाषैरनुदिनमभितः पीडितो दुःख सर्वे।
क्षन्तव्यो मेपराधः प्रकटित वदने कामरूपे कराले॥

कालाम्रांश्यामलाङ्गी व्विडलितचिकुरा खड्गमुण्डाभिरामः।
न्यास त्राणेष्टदात्रीम् कुण पगणशिरो मालिनीन्दीर्घ नेत्राम्॥
संसारस्यैक साराम्भव जन नहराम्भावितोभावनाभिः।
क्षन्तव्यो मेपराधः प्रकटित वदने कामरूपे कराले॥

ब्रह्मा विष्णु स्तथेशः परिणमति सदा त्वत्पदाम्भोज युक्त।
म्भाग्याभावान्न चाहम्भव जननि भवत्पाद युग्मम्भजामि॥
नित्यंल्लोभ प्रलोभैः कृतविशमतिः कामुकस्त्वाम्प्रयाषे।
क्षन्तव्यो मेपराधः प्रकटित वदने कामरूपे कराले।

रागद्वैषः प्रमत्तः कलुष युत तनुः कामनाभोग लुब्धः।
कार्य्याकार्य्या विचारी कुलमति रहितः कौलसंधैर्विहीनः॥
क्वधयान्ते क्वचार्च्चा च्चमनुजपनन्नैव किञ्चत् कृतोहम्।
क्षन्तव्यो मेपराधः प्रकटित वदने कामरूपे कराले॥

रोगीः दुःखी दरिद्रः परकशकृपणः पांशुल्लः पापचेता।
निद्रालस्य प्रसक्तारसुजठरमणे व्याकुलः कल्पितात्मा॥
किन्ने पूजा विधानन्त्वयिक्वचनुमतिः क्वानुराग क्वचास्था।
क्षन्तव्यो मेपराधः प्रकटित वदने कामरूपे कराले॥

मिथ्या व्यामोह रागैः परिवृतमनसः क्लेश संधान्वितस्य।
क्षुन्निद्रोधान्वितस्य स्मरण विरहिणः पापकर्म्म प्रवृत्तैः॥
दारिद्रयस्य क्वधर्मः क्वचजननिरुचिः क्वस्थिस्साधु सधैः।
क्षन्तव्योमेपराधः प्रकटित वदने कामरूपे कराले॥

मातस्तातस्यदेहाज्जननि जठरगः संस्थितस्त्वद्वशेहन्।
त्व हर्त्रा कारयित्रीकर गुणमयी कर्महेतु स्वरूपा॥
त्वम्बुद्धिश्चित संस्थाप्यमहति भवती सर्व्वमेतत्क्षमस्व।
क्षन्तव्यो मेपराधः प्रकटित वदने कामरूपे कराले॥

तवम्भूमिस्त्वञ्जलञ्च त्वमसि हुतबहस्त्वञ्जगद्वायुरूपा।
त्वञ्चाकाशम्भनश्च प्रकृतिरसि महत्पूर्व्विका पूर्व्वपूर्व्वा॥
आत्मात्वञ्चासिमातः परिमसिभवती त्वत्परन्नैव किञ्चित्।
क्षन्तव्योमेपराधः प्रकटित वदने कामरूपे कराले॥

Nte Naivedyaikakanchd Kwachidapi Na Kritam Naapebhavon Bhaktih
Vasyaasi Naiva Poojapa Na Cha Guna Kothanam Naapio Charchaa-Kriteeta
Kshanta Vyo. . .

Jaanami Twan Na Chaaham Bhava Bhayaharaneem Sarvasiddhi Pradaatrim
Nnivya Wandd Dyaadyaa Tya Gunamayee Ninitaya Shudhodadhadyam ।
Mithya Karmma Bhilashei Ranudinmbhitah Peedito Dukkha Sarve
Kshantavyo. . .

Kalamraashyaam Laangee Vivdalita Chikura Kadagmundaniram
Nyaas Traaneshtdaatrreem Kuna Paganashiro Maalini Ndeergh Nekaam
Sansarasyeka Saramphava Jan NaharamBha Vitobhav Naabhih
Kshan Tavyo Meparadhe. . .

Brahma Viushnu Sthteshah PParanimati Sada Twatpadaambhoj Yuktai
Mbhagyabhavanna Chaahambhavam JananiBhavatpaad Yugmambhaja Mili
Nityati Lubha Pralobheih Kritavishmatih Rahitah Kaulsandheir Viheenahu
Kwadhayaante Kwachararchcha Chchamanuj Panneiva Kinchita Kritohami
Kshantavya Me Paraadhi. . .

Raagadveshah Pramattah Kalush Yuta Tanuh Kamanabhog Lubdhai
Karyakarya Vichari Kulamati Rahitah Kaulsandheirvihee Nahi
Kwadhayaante Kwachschchaarcha Chchamanujapanneiva Kinchi Ta Kutoham
Kshantavya Meparaadhe . . .
Mithya Vyaamoha Ragei Parivritmanasah Klesh Sandhanvita Sya
Kshunni Drodhanvitasya Smaran Virhani Papkarnn Pravritteih
Daaridragasya Kwadharmah Kwach Jani Ruchih

त्वंकाली त्वञ्चतारात्वमसि गिरिसुता सुन्दरी भैरवीत्वम्।
त्वन्दुर्गा छिन्नमस्ता त्वमसि चभवना त्वम्हिलक्ष्मीः शिवात्वम्॥
धूमा मातंगि नीत्वन्त्मसि च बगला मंगलादिस्तवाख्या।
क्षन्तव्यो मेपराधः प्रकटित वदने कामरूपे कराले॥

स्तोत्रेणानेन देवोम्परिणमति जनो यः सदाभक्ति युक्तो।
दुष्कृत्यादुर्गा संधम्परितरति शतं विघ्नतानाशमेति॥
नाविर्व्वाधिः कदाचित्भवति यदि पुनस्सर्वदा सापराधः।
स्सर्त्वन्तत्कामरूपे त्रिभुवन जननि क्षामेय पुत्रबुद्धया॥

ज्ञाता वक्ता कवीशोभवति धनपतिर्दानशीलो दयात्वा।
निः पापी निः कलंकी कुलपति कुशलस्सत्यवाग्धार्म्मिकश्च॥
नित्यानन्दो दयाऽयः पशुगणिविमुखस्सत्पथा चारुशीलः।
संसाराब्धि सुकेन प्रतिरति गिरिजा पादयुग्मा बलम्बात्॥

Kwasthissaadhu Sangheit
Kshantavya Meparaadhe. . .

Matastaatatasyadehajjanani Jatharagah SansthiTa
Tastwa Dwashe Han
Kshunnidrodha Anvitasya Smaran Virahanih Paap Karma
Pravritteh
Daardragasya Kwadharmah Kwathajani Ruchih Kwasthi
Saadhu Sagheihi
Kshantavya Me Paraadhe. . .

Tavambhumistvaanjalancha Twamasi Hutabahst Dan
Jagadwayu Roopa
Twanchaakaasham Bhanascha Prakritirasi
Mahatpoorvvika Poorvapoorva
Aatmaa twanchabsi Maatah Parimasi Bhavati
twatparnneiva Kinchit
Kshantavya Me Paraadhe . . .

Twamkaali Twancha Taara Twamasi Girisuta Sundari
Bhairavi Tware
Twan Durga Chhinamasta Twamasi Chabhavana
Twamahilakhih Shivatwam
Dhama Maatingi Neetwantmasi Cha Bagald
Mangaladistvaakhya
Kshantavya Me Paraadhe. . .

Strotrena Nena Devomparinamati Jano Yah Sadabhoki
Yukto
Dushkrityadurga Sandhamparitarati Shatam
Vvignataanaa Shameti
Naavivrvaadhi Kadachita Bhavani Yadi Punssarvada
Saaparaadah
Sstrvantat Kaam Roope Tribvhoovan Janani Khaameya
Putra Buddhyada

Gyaata Vaktaa Kaveeshobhavat, Dhanapatirdansheero
Dayaatwaai
Nih Paapi Nih Kalanki Kulapati Kukhalssatya Vaagdharmi
Kashcha
Nityaanando Dayaayah Pashuganivimukhassatpatha
Chaaru Sheelah
Sansaaraabhdi Sukena Prati Rati Girija Paadyugmaa
Valambaat | |

अथ देव्यपराधक्षमापन स्तोत्रम्

न मंत्रं नो यंत्रं तदपि च न जाने स्तुतिमहो।
न चाह्वानं ध्यानं तदपि च न जाने स्तुति कथा।।
न जाने मुद्रास्ते तदपि च न जाने विलपनम्।
पर जाने मातस्त्वदनुसरणं क्लेश हरणम्।।
विधेरज्ञानेन द्रविणं विरहेणालसतया।
विधेया शक्यत्वात्तव चरणयोर्याच्युतिरभूत्।।
तदेतत्क्षन्तव्यं जननि! सकलोद्धारिणी शिवे।
कुपुत्रो जायेत क्वचिदपि कुमाता न भवति।।
पृथिव्यां पुत्रास्थे जननि ! बहवः सन्ति सरलाः।
परं तेषां मध्ये विरल तरलोऽहं तव सुतः।।
मदीयोयं त्यागः समुचितमिदं नो तव शिवे।
कुपुत्रो जायेत क्वचिदपि कुमाता न भवति।।
जगन्मातर्मातस्तव चरण सेवा न रचिता।
न वा दत्तं देवि ! द्रविणमपि भूयस्तव मया।।
तथापि त्वं स्नेहं मयि निरूपं यत्प्रकुरुषे।
कुपुत्रो जायेत क्वचिदपि कुमाता न भवति।।
परित्यक्ता देवाविविधि विधसेवा कुलतया।
मया पंचाशीतेरधिकमपनीते तु वयसि।।
इदानीं चेन्मातस्त्व यदि कृपानापि भविता।
निरालम्बो लम्बोदर जननि ! कं यामि शरणम्।।
श्वपाको जल्पाको भवति मधुपाकोपमगिरा।
निरातंको रंको विहरति चिरं कोटि कनकैः।।
तवापर्णे कर्णे विशति मनु वर्णे फलमिदम्।
जनः को जानीते जननि ! जपनीयं जप विधौ।।
चिताभस्मा लेपो गरलमशनं दिक्पटधरो।
जटाधारी कण्ठे भुजग पतिहारी पशुपतिः।।

Devya Aparaadh Kshamaapan Strotra

(An Apology to the Goddess)

Na Mantram no yantram tadapi cha na jaane stutimaho |
Na Chaavahnam Dhyanam Tadapi Cha Na Jaane Stuti Kathah ||
Na Jaane Mudraaste Tadap Cha Na Jane Vilapanam |
Param Jane Matastwadanusarbnam Klesh Haranam ||
Vidheragyaanema Dravina VirahenaLasatayaa |
Vidheyaa Shakya Twaattva Charana Yoprya Chyutir Bhoot ||
Tadetamtkshantavyam Janani Sakaloddhaarini Shive |
Kuputro Jaayeta Kwachidapi Kumaata Na Bhavati ||
Prathivyaam Putraaste Janani Vah Vah Santi Saralah |
Param Tesham Madhye Viral Taraleeaham Tav Sutah ||
Nadiyoyan Tyagah Samvehijamidam No Tab Shive |
Kuputro Jayeta Kwachidapi Kumaataa Na Bhavati ||
Jagatmaatarmatas Tava Charan Sewa Na Rachita |
Na Wa Dattam Devi Dravi Namapi Bhuyastwa Mayaa ||
Tathaapi Twam Sneham Mayi Nirupamam Yatprakurushe |
Kurutro Jayeta Kwachidapi Kumaata Na Bhavati ||
Parityakta Devanvividhi Vidhi Sewa Kulataya |
Maya Panchasheete Radhiko Mapaneete Tu Vayasi ||
Idaani Chetmatastva Yadi Kripanaapi Bhavita |
Niralambo Lambovara Janani Kam Yaami Sharanam ||
Swapaako Jalpaako Bhavati Madhupaakopamagira |
Niratanko Ranko Viharati Chiram Koti Kanakeih ||
Tavaaparne Karne Vishati Manu Varne Phalamidam |
Janah Ki Jaaneete Janani Japaneeyam Japavidhaud ||
Chita Bhasma Lepo Garalamashanam Dikpatdharo |
Jatadhaari Kanthe Bhujag Patihaari Pashupatih ||
Kapaali Bhootesho Bhajati Jagdeesheikpadaveen |
Bhavaani Twatpaani Grihan Paripaati Phalamidam ||
Na Mokshasyaakaanksha Bhaya Vibhav Vaanchapi Chan Me |

कपाली भूतेशो भजति जगदीशैकपदवीं।
भवानि त्वत्पाणि ग्रहण परिपाटी फलमिदम्।
न मोक्षस्याकांक्षा भव विभव वांछापि च न मे।
न विज्ञानापेक्षा शशिमुखि सुखेच्छापि न पुनः॥
अतस्त्वां संयाचे जननि ! जननं यातु मम वै।
मृडानी रुद्राणी शिव ! शिव ! भवानीति जपतः॥
नाराधितासि विधिना विविधोपचारैः।
किं रुक्ष चिन्तनपरैर्नकृतं वचोभिः॥
श्यामे त्वमेव यदि किंचन मय्यनाथे।
धत्से कृपामुचितमम्ब। परं तवैव॥
आपत्सु मग्नः स्मरणं त्वदीयं करोमि दुर्गे ! करुणार्णवेशि।
नैतच्छठत्वं मम भावयेथाः क्षुधातृषार्ता जननीं स्मरन्ति॥
जगदम्ब विचित्रमत्र किं परिपूर्णा करुणास्ति चेन्मयि।
अपराध परंपरापरं नहि माता समुपेक्षते सुतम्॥
मत्समः पातकी नास्ति पापघ्नीः त्वत्समा न हि।
एवं ज्ञात्वा महादेवि! यथायोग्यं तथा कुरु॥

□□□

Na Vigyaana Peksha Shashimukha Sukhe chchhaapi Na
Punah | |
Atastwam Sanyaache Janani Jananam Yatu Mam Vei |
Mridaani Rudraani Shiv-Shiv Bhavaniti Mam Japatah | |
Naraadhitaasi Vidhinaa Vividhopa Chaare |
Kim Ruksha Chintansha Reirnakritam Vachobhih | |
Shyaame Twameva Yadi Kinchan Mayyanathi
   Dhatse Kripamuchi Tamba Param Taveiva
Aapatsu Magnah Smaranam Twadeeyam
  Burge! Karvnarnaveshi |

Jagadamba Vichitrah Matra Kimparipoorna
   Karunarstika Chanmeyi | |
Naitachhathatvam Mam Bhavaye Thah
   Kshvdha Trishaarta Janani Smarant |
Aparaadh Pamramparavritam Nahi Mata
   Samupekhate Sutam |
Matsam, Paataki, Naasti
   Rapdaghni Twatsama Nahi
Evam Gyaatvam Mahadevi
   Yathayogyam Ta Tha Kuru | |

             ☐☐☐

श्रीमहाकाली चालीसा

जय काली कंकाल मालिनी।
जय मंगला महा कपालिनी।।

रक्तबीज वध कारिणी माता।
सदा भक्तन के सुखदाता।।

शिरो मालिका भूषित अंगे।
जय काली मधु मध्य मतंगे।।

हर हृदयारविंद सुविलासिनी।
जय जगदम्ब सकलदुचनाशिनी।।

ह्रीं काली श्रीं महा कराली।
क्रीं कल्याणी दक्षिण काली।।

जय कलावती जय विद्यावती।
जय तारा सुन्दरी महामती।।

देहु सुबुद्धि हरहु सब संकट।
होहु भक्त के आगे प्रकट।।

जय ओंकारे जय हुंकारे।
महाशक्ति जय अपरम्पारे।।

कमला कलियुग दर्प विनाशिनी।
सदा भक्तजन के भय नाशिनी।।

अब जगदम्ब न देर लगावहु।
दुख दरिद्रता मोर हटावहु।।

जयति कराल काल के माता।
कालानल समान धुति गाता।।

Shree Mahakali Chaleesa

Jai kali kankaala maalini
Jai mangala maha kapaalini
Rakta beeja vadha kaarinee mata
Sada bhakten ke sukhadata
Shiro maalika bhooshita ange
Jai kail madhu Madhya matange
Har bridyearvinda suvibasini
Jai jagadamba sakala dukhaneashini
Heem kali saree maha karaali
Kreem kalyani Dakshine kali
Jai kalavati jai vidyavati
Jai tara sundani matamati
Dehu serbuddhi harahu sat sankat
Hohu bhakat ke aage prekati
Jai Onkaare jai hunkeere
Mahashapti jai aparampaare
Kamala kaliyug darka vinaashini
Sada bhaktan ke bhaya naashini
Aba jagadamb na deva laga vahu
Dukh daridvata mora hata vahu
Jayati kavaala kaal ke maata
Kalaanal samaan dhuti gaata
Jai shankari surashi sanaatani
Kota siddhapavi maatu puratani
Kapardini kali kalmash mochani
Jai vikasita nava nalin vilochani
Ananda aananda midhanaa
Dehu Maatu mohi nirmala gyaana
Karunnamnita saagar kripsamayi
Hohn duslita jana par ab mirdayi
Sakala eeva tohi samaan pyaara
Sakala vishwa tore aahaara
Pralaya kaal me nartan kaamini
Jaga jananu sab jag ke paalini

जय शंकरी सुरशि सनातनि।
कोटि सिद्धकवि मातु पुरातनि।।

कपर्दिनी कलि कल्मष मोचनि।
जय विकसित नव नलिन विलोचनि।।

आनन्दा आनन्द निधाना।
देहु मातु मोहि निर्मल ज्ञाना।।

करुणामृत सागर कृपामयी।
होहु दुष्टजन पर अब निर्दयी।।

सकल जीव तोहि समान प्यारा।
सकल विश्व तोरे अहारा।।

प्रलय काल में नर्त्तन कारिणि।
जगजननि सब जग के पालिनी।।

महोदरी माहेश्वरि माया।
हिमगिरी सुता विश्व की छाया।।

स्वच्छच्छरत् मराद् धुनि माहीं।
गर्जत तूहि और कोउ नाहीं।।

यह चालीसा जो जन गावे।
मातु भक्त वांछित फल पावे।।

केला और फल फूल चढ़ावे।
मांस खून नहीं छुवावे।।

सबके तुम समान महतारी।
काहे कोई बकरा को मारी।

सब जीवों के जीव में, व्यापक तू ही अम्ब।
कहत सिद्ध कवि सब जगत, तौर सुत जगदम्ब।।

Mahodari maaheshwari maya
Himgiri suta vishwa ki chhaya
Swachchacha rad maradi dhuni maaheen
Garjat tooh aur koi naahem
Yeh Chaaluse jo jana gave
Matu bhakta vaanchita phala pave
Kela aur phala phool;a chaddaava
Maansa aur khoon nahin chn vaave
Sabake tum saman mahatami
Kahe koyi bahera ko maani

Sab jeevon ke jeeva mein
Vyapaka too hi amba
Kahata siddha kani sab jagat
Tere suta Jagadamba||

Vikram Samvat Unnersa san
Vyaasi mein mam hanma|
Chooha wali putra hoon
Sthaan Gayaapur dhama||

श्रीमहाकाली की आरती

अम्बे तू है जगदम्बे काली, जय दुर्गे खप्पर वाली,
तेरे ही गुण गावें भारती, ओ मैया! हम सब उतारें तेरी आरती।

तेरे भक्तजनों पर मैया, भीड़ पड़ी है भारी,
दानवदल पर टूट पड़ो मां, करके सिंह सवारी।

सौ सौ सिंहों से तू बलशाली, अष्ट भुजाओं वाली,
दुष्टों को तू ही ललकारती, ओ मैया! हम सब उतारें तेरी आरती।

मां-बेटे का है इस जग में, बड़ा ही निर्मल नाता,
पूत कपूत सुने हैं पर ना, माता सुनी कुमाता।

सब पे करुणा दर्शाने वाली, अमृत बरसाने वाली,
दुखियों के दुखड़े निवारती, ओ मैया! हम सब उतारें तेरी आरती।

नहीं मांगते धन और दौलत, न चांदी न सोना,
हम तो मांगें मां तेरे मन में, इक छोटा सा कोना।

सबकी बिगड़ी बनाने वाली, लाज बचाने वाली,
सतियों के सत को संवारती, ओ मैया! हम सब उतारें तेरी आरती।

चरण-शरण में खड़े तुम्हारी, ले पूजा की थाली,
वरद हस्त सिर पर रख दो, मां संकट हरने वाली।

मैया भर दो भक्ति रस प्याली, अष्ट भुजाओं वाली,
भक्तों के कारज, तू ही सारती, ओ मैया! हम सब उतारें तेरी आरती।

Aarti: Maan Kaali Ki

Ambe too hai jagadamba kali, Jai Durge khappar wali
Tere her guna gaaven bhaarati, O Maiyya,
Ham sab utaaren teri aarati I

Tere bhakta jano per maiyya, Bhuda pari hai bhaari
Daanavadala per toota paro maan, Karaki siisa sawaami

Sare sinhon se too balashaali, Ashtabhujaaon waali
Dushton ko too her lalakaarati, O Mayya
Ham saba utaaren tari aarati I

Maan beta ka hai is jaga men, Bada her mirmal naata
Poota kapoota sune hain per na, Maata suni Kumaataa

Sab par karuna darshana wali, Amrita barasaane waali
Dukhiyon ke dukhdi nivaarati, O Mayya
Ham saba utaaren tari aarati I

Nahin maangati dhan an daulat, Na chandi na sona
Ham to maange maan tere mana men, Ik chhota sa kona

Sabaki bigadee banana wali, Laaj bachaane wali
Satiyou ke sata ko sanwaarati, O Maiyya
Ham saba utaaren tari aarati I

Charan-sharan men ptade tumhaari, Le pooja ki thaali
Varada hasta sir par rakh do, Maan sankata harane waali

Maiyya bhar do bhakti rasa ki pyaali,
Ashta bhujeaon waali
Bhakto ke kaaraj too her saarati
O Maiyya
Ham saba utaaren tari aarati I

❑❑❑